应用技术型高等教育"十二五"规划教材
（机械设计制造及其自动化专业课程群系列）

先进制造技术
（双语版）

主　编　宋庭新
副主编　刘　顿　胡晓菊
参　编　周　伟　程　涛　王林琳　娄德元　杨奇彪
英文校核　［英］Peter Bennett

内容提要

本书从大量的英文原文中选取了一些典型的先进制造技术作为主要内容,并且对正文中出现的英语生词和专业词汇进行了汉语标注,适合用作双语教学。

本书围绕先进制造技术的各个主题,介绍了先进制造工艺与材料、制造自动化技术、现代生产管理技术和先进制造模式四个方面的内容,不仅包含了传统的先进制造技术,也包含了目前新兴的一些先进制造方法。全书共分为19章,包括超精密加工和高速加工技术、激光加工技术、3D打印技术、先进材料技术、计算机辅助设计与制造、柔性制造系统、计算机集成制造系统、制造资源计划、制造执行系统、精益生产、敏捷制造等内容。

本书可以作为机械工程、工业工程、仪器仪表等专业本科生和研究生的双语教学教材和专业英语教材,也可以作为科研和工程技术人员的参考书。

图书在版编目(CIP)数据

先进制造技术:双语版 / 宋庭新主编. -- 北京:中国水利水电出版社,2014.8
 应用技术型高等教育"十二五"规划教材. 机械设计制造及其自动化专业课程群系列
 ISBN 978-7-5170-2164-3

Ⅰ. ①先… Ⅱ. ①宋… Ⅲ. ①机械制造工艺—双语教学—高等学校—教材 Ⅳ. ①TH16

中国版本图书馆CIP数据核字(2014)第131216号

策划编辑:宋俊娥 责任编辑:李 炎 封面设计:李 佳

书　名	应用技术型高等教育"十二五"规划教材 (机械设计制造及其自动化专业课程群系列) **先进制造技术(双语版)**
作　者	主　编 宋庭新　副主编 刘　顿　胡晓菊
出版发行	中国水利水电出版社 (北京市海淀区玉渊潭南路1号D座 100038) 网　址:www.waterpub.com.cn E-mail:mchannel@263.net(万水) 　　　　sales@waterpub.com.cn 电　话:(010)68367658(发行部)、82562819(万水)
经　售	北京科水图书销售中心(零售) 电话:(010)88383994、63202643、68545874 全国各地新华书店和相关出版物销售网点
排　版	北京万水电子信息有限公司
印　刷	三河市鑫金马印装有限公司
规　格	184mm×260mm 16开本 10.25印张 207千字
版　次	2014年8月第1版 2014年8月第1次印刷
印　数	0001—3000册
定　价	19.00元

凡购买我社图书,如有缺页、倒页、脱页的,本社发行部负责调换

版权所有·侵权必究

前　言

目前国内很多高校都在推广双语教学，这不仅让学生掌握了专业知识，同时也学习到了专业英语词汇。特别是在很多高校取消了专业英语课程的情况下，双语教学在某种程度上也承担着专业英语教学的任务。《先进制造技术》是一门很适合机械类专业作为双语教学的课程。本书在参考国内外众多英文原版教材和文章的基础上，根据目前先进制造技术的发展现状，选编了一些典型的英文材料作为本书的内容。

先进制造技术在传统制造技术的基础上融合了信息技术、自动控制技术和现代生产管理理念等内容，所涉及的领域非常广泛，学科跨度大。本书围绕先进制造技术的各个主题，介绍了先进制造工艺与材料、制造自动化技术、现代生产管理技术和先进制造模式四个方面的内容，不仅包含了传统的先进制造技术，也包含了目前新兴的一些先进制造方法。全书共分为 19 个章节，分别由胡晓菊编写第 1、7 章，刘顿编写第 2、3、4 章，娄德元编写第 5 章，程涛编写第 6、8、11 章，周伟编写第 9、15 章，杨奇彪编写第 10 章，王林琳编写第 12、13、14 章，宋庭新编写第 16、17、18、19 章。本书由宋庭新担任主编，Peter Bennett 担任英文校核。

作为一本双语教材，本书在编排上力争突出自己的特色。对于正文中出现的英语生词都进行了汉语标注，插图和图表文字均为中英对照，以保证学生可以流畅地阅读本书。同时把每一章所涉及的本领域专业英语词汇列在章节的后面，便于学生系统地学习掌握专业词汇。由于编者专业知识的局限性和时间仓促，在编译的过程中难免出现一些失误，欢迎广大读者批评指正（邮箱 songtx2006@163.com）。

本书可以作为机械工程、工业工程、仪器仪表等专业的本科生和研究生的双语教学教材和专业英语教材，也可以作为科研和工程技术人员的参考书。

编者
2014 年 7 月

Contents
目录

Part I Advanced Manufacturing Process and Materials
先进制造工艺与材料···1

Chapter 1 Ultra-precision Machining and High Speed Machining
超精密加工和高速加工技术··2

Chapter 2 Laser Processing Technology
激光加工技术··10

Chapter 3 3D Printing
3D 打印技术··24

Chapter 4 Nanofabrication Technology
纳米加工技术··29

Chapter 5 Advanced Materials Technology
先进材料技术··34

Part II Manufacturing Automation Technology
制造自动化技术···38

Chapter 6 CAD/CAM/CAE/CAPP
计算机辅助设计/制造/工程/工艺规划································39

Chapter 7 Modern CNC Machining Technology
现代数控加工技术··44

Chapter 8 Flexible Manufacturing System
柔性制造系统··53

Chapter 9 Computer Integrated Manufacturing System
计算机集成制造系统··60

Chapter 10 Industrial Robot Technology
工业机器人技术··71

Chapter 11 Automatic Detection and Monitoring Technology
自动检测与监控技术··79

Part III Modern Production and Management Technology
现代生产管理技术 ·· 85

Chapter 12 Product Data Management
产品数据管理 ·· 86

Chapter 13 Manufacturing Resource Planning
制造资源计划 ·· 91

Chapter 14 Enterprise Resource Planning
企业资源计划 ·· 102

Chapter 15 Manufacturing Execution Systems
制造执行系统 ·· 107

Part IV Advanced Manufacturing Mode
先进制造模式 ·· 116

Chapter 16 Lean Production
精益生产 ·· 117

Chapter 17 Agile Manufacturing
敏捷制造 ·· 126

Chapter 18 Remanufacturing
再制造 ·· 140

Chapter 19 Green Manufacturing
绿色制造 ·· 148

参考文献 ·· 156

Part I

Advanced Manufacturing Process and Materials

先进制造工艺与材料

Chapter 1　Ultra-precision Machining and High Speed Machining 超精密加工和高速加工技术

1. Finishing Operations　精加工

1.1 Honing　珩磨

Honing is an operation used primarily to give holes a fine surface finish. The honing tool consists of a set of aluminum-oxide or silicon-carbide bonded abrasives called stones. They are mounted on a mandrel that rotates in the hole, applying a radial force with a reciprocating axial motion, this action produces across-hatched problem. The stones can be adjusted radically for different hole sizes. Honing is also done on external cylindrical or flat surfaces and to remove sharp edges on cutting tools and inserts. Fig. 1.1 is a schematic illustration of a honing tool used to improve the surface finish of bored or ground holes.

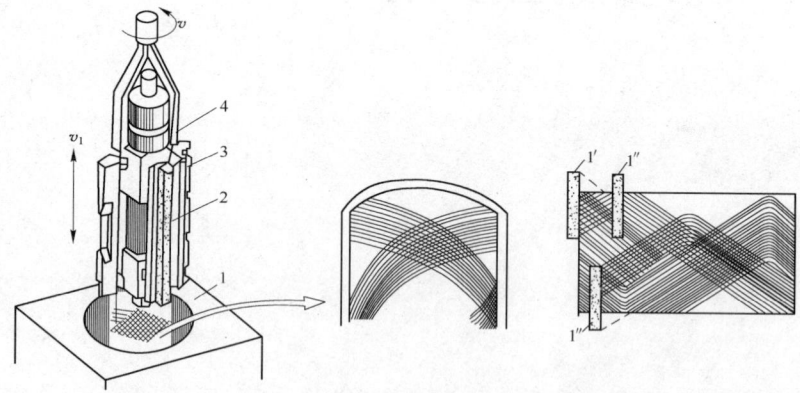

Fig. 1.1　The cutting locus of honing head and honing oilstone
1-work piece; 2-honing stick; 3-grinding flat; 4-shaft coupling

The fineness of surface finish can be controlled by the type and size of abrasive used, the pressure applied, and speed. Surface speeds range from about 45m/min to 90m/min. A fluid is used to remove chips and to keep temperatures low. If not done properly, honing can produce holes that are neither straight nor cylindrical, but with shapes that are bell-mouthed or tapered.

1.2 Super-finishing 超精加工

In super-finishing the pressure applied is very light and the motion of the stone has a short stroke. The process is controlled so that the grains do not travel along the same path on the surface of the work piece being finished. Fig. 1.2 is the schematic illustrations of the super-finishing process for a cylindrical part.

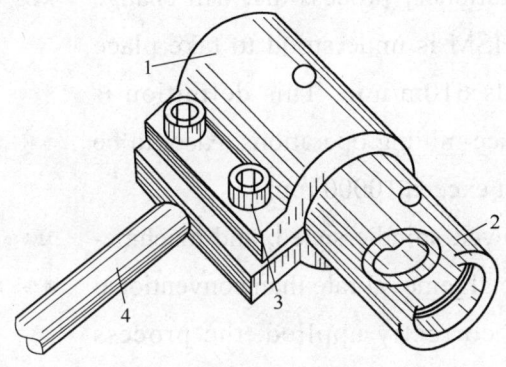

Fig. 1.2 A tool for grind excircle
1-jacket; 2-grind jacket; 3-adjusting screw; 4-hand shank

1.3 Lapping 精研

Lapping is a finishing operation used on flat or cylindrical surfaces. The lap is usually made of cast iron, copper, leather, or cloth. The abrasive particles are embedded in the lap, or they maybe carried through a slurry. Depending on the hardness of the work piece, lapping pressures range from 7kPa to 140kPa. Dimensional tolerances on the order of ±0.0004 to ei can be obtained with the use of fine abrasives up to grit size 900. Surface finish can be as smooth as 0.025μm to 0.1μm.

1.4 Polishing 抛光

Polishing is a process that produces a smooth surface finish. Two basic mechanisms are involved in the polishing process: (a) fine-scale abrasive removal; (b) softening and smearing of surface layers by frictional heating during polishing. The shiny appearance of polished surfaces results from the smearing action.

Polishing is done with disks or belts made of fabric, leather etc that are coated with fine powders of aluminum oxide or diamond. Parts with irregular shapes, sharp corners, and sharp projections are difficult to polish.

2. High-Speed Machining 高速加工

Most of the time, any process which employ a spindle that can operate at high rpm is labeled HSM. In fact, like the introduction of NC and later CNC, HSM is a revolutionary process that will change the way metal removal. Usually, HSM is understood to take place when cutter surface speed exceeds 610m/min. This definition is based on single-point turning and face-milling operations. Also, to be considered HSM, spindle speed must exceed 10000 rpm.

The combination of spindle power, spindle speed, and machine-axis feed rates produces a greater metal removal rate than conventional metal cutting technology. When correctly applied, the process optimizes all the factors involved in the cutting operation by applying methods that fully exploit the machine's performance. It creates a perfect balance of all parameters that control metal removal.

The final goal of firms that build high-speed machining systems is to deliver reliable and sustainable solutions with improved processes and performance, reduced production time, greatly reduced hand finishing, improved quality, and lower production cost.

Before introducing HSM, machine tool builders have to consider a number of important factors including: weight of mobile components, center of gravity, rigidity/stability, axis drives, CNC, accuracy, machine configuration, machine programming, training and maintenance.

Weight of the moving components of the system is the most important criterion. Mobile parts need not only to move rapidly, but to obtain the maximum possible acceleration in the minimum distance. In the case of a wide, tall machine, acceleration is the enemy and causes the machine to tip up. To eliminate this problem, the center of gravity must be at the lowest possible position.

Rigidity/stability is the key to HSM. A system that is not rigid produces poor results, and may cause a real disaster. Chatter, surface finish, and accuracy, as well as tool, spindle, and machine life all depend upon system rigidity.

Developing and fabricating a large, high-speed machine caused a company to revise the traditional conception of a machine, particularly of the driving system and of the weight of mobile components. The classical ball screws and nuts, racks and pinions, and gearboxes created worries.

Linear motors are the only way to solve the problem. Installing linear motors eliminate all intermediary parts such as belt drives, gearboxes, ball screws, and pinions, which are not very rigid. The linear motors permit more accurate calculation of the required parameters.

It is necessary to protect the linear motors against dust and contaminants, and to develop a cooling system and heat transfer for the machine structures.

In spite of high feed rates, high acceleration, a relatively light machine, and part geometry, the HSM system has to provide very good positioning accuracy and repeatability. The feedback measurement devices used, such as linear scales and lasers, bare directly mounted on the axis. In addition to the accuracy aspect, the laser feedback system also makes it possible to automatically change the machine axis position as temperature fluctuates. In other words, the cutter follows the part movements driven by thermal effects. This capability is important because all machine tool builders would like to install their equipment in a building that has a temperature control system.

What are the basic requirements for HSM? Many factors influence the performance of high-speed machines. They must be balanced to optimize the final results. As a rule, performance improves when chatter is eliminated. It's easiest to remove chatter when all the elements in the process combine to produce a system with high rigidity.

For many years, HSM is considered a process only suited for

light-duty finishing operations. In fact, many of the machines now in operation are still used for this limited part of the production process. This situation is gradually changing. Pressure to use HSM has come, in particular, from the aerospace industry's need to produce structural monolithic components in aluminum. In that field, HSM has been adopted as a process able to produce a part from rough to finish using the same machine.

Much information on HSM involves aluminum, but what about the other metals? Machine tool builders, software developers, and in particular, cutting-tool makers offer a spectrum of products. Unique problems abound when machining harder.

With harder to machine materials, such as heat-resistant alloys, the tool spends more time in one location, compared to aluminum. Therefore, there is more heat generation and more pressure on the workpiece that might cause adverse deformation. This is very critical in complex or thin cross sections.

Coolant for HSM operations is a controversial issue. Dry, mist, and flood cooling are all used. The problem is that, at present, there is through the tool no way to get coolant to the actual cutting surface, even with very high pressure, through the tool delivery systems. So the coolant in all cases has only peripheral influence on tool and workpiece temperature.

For machining of 50 HRC metals, which is called hard machining, air cooling is recommended to avoid thermal shock. Below that hardness, high-speed roughing and finishing is almost dry machining. The only exceptions are gummy materials, like aluminum or some stainless steel. Compressed air, or an oil mist in an air stream, is recommended to move the chips, not fluids that can cause thermal cracking of the tool coating. Mist coolant is used sometimes when you need a very low surface roughness. It's used for the lubricant properties, not for the heat dissipation quality.

In die and mold machining, it's recommended to run dry to avoid thermal shock to the cutting tool. For applications in heat-resistant materials, such as titanium, heavy volumes of coolant are recommended to avoid chemical and abrasive wear at high speed. At the same time, the tendency for some thermal cracks must be accepted.

The latest tool designs represent a change in philosophy from multilayer coatings to a single nanocoat about 0.001μm thick. This design gives longer tool life because it has a 75% lower coefficient of friction than TiAlN and is three times harder. With this lubricity there is less heat, and less oxidation and wear. It can handle materials up to 80 HRC and tool life can be increased 5 to 10 times. Coatings may or may not be an advantage. For example, in aerospace work, you cannot use a coating that contains aluminum on titanium because of contamination problems. But generally, cutting tools used on all heat-resistant alloys use coatings.

Machine tools made specifically for HSM have some unique features. In evaluating these designs, when it comes to HSM of harder materials, machines can feed faster than tools can cut. Speeds of 610 to 914m/min are possible in aluminum, but with steel of 50 HRC, 122 to 137m/min are more common. You can achieve a chip load of 0.5 – 1.3mm per tooth with aluminum, but 0.08 – 0.2mm in hard steel is more standard. Chip load is the driving force when it comes to machining harder materials.

It's finally clear that HSM is a viable production process with capabilities beyond the finishing area, and that the limits of the metal removal rate achieved by HSM are determined by a series of factors linked to the performance limitations of all the elements involved in HSM. These elements include:

(1) The machine. High feed rate is not sufficient. It must be complemented by high structural rigidity, high acceleration/deceleration, and a CNC capable of supporting the machine's enhanced performance.

(2) Spindle. High rpm is not all that's needed to produce a high metal removal rate. High power, high torque, and rigidity are required to ensure improved tool life and good surface finish.

(3) Cutters. While very good solutions are available for materials like aluminum, the cutters still make it difficult to achieve a dramatic breakthrough in the machining of exotic materials, like titanium and inconel, at high speed. In some cases, cutter substantially influences part-production costs. This point emphasizes the importance of cutting

tests and cost studies before making any decisions about adopting HSM.

(4) <u>Fixturing</u>. Fixturing is very often the weakest link in the system. If the fixture is not rigid enough to avoid chatter during the cutting process, the most rigid and dynamic machine, equipped with a powerful spindle and the proper tooling, is worthless. 夹具

(5) <u>Human resource</u>. Human resource is probably the most important factor in the successful application of HSM. It's often ignored, leading to disappointing results. Users must select the right <u>individuals</u> to program, operate, and manage the HSM installation, and it's also important to give them the training and support them to implement the new technology. 人力资源

个人

专业词汇

honing 珩磨
lapping 精研
super-finishing 超精加工
finish 光洁度
polishing 抛光
workpiece 工件
fixturing 夹具
cutting tools 刀具
chips 切屑
parts 零件
components 零部件
tolerance 公差
process 工艺
turning 车削
milling 铣削
boring 镗孔
feed 进给
rigidity 刚度
stability 稳定性

chatter 颤动
ball screws 滚珠丝杠
nut 螺母
rack 齿条
pinion 齿轮
machine tools 机床
spindle 主轴
heat-resistant 耐热的
alloy 合金
coolant 冷却剂
tool coating 刀具涂层
lubricity 润滑
die and mold 模具
wear 磨损
chip load 进刀量
coefficient of friction 摩擦系数
gearbox 齿轮箱
production cost 生产成本

思考题：

1. 请说明珩磨、精研和抛光的区别。
2. 什么是高速加工？它的特点是什么？
3. 刚度和稳定性为什么对于高速加工非常重要？
4. 在高速加工中如何选择冷却剂？
5. 哪些因素限制了高速加工的切削效率？

Chapter 2 Laser Processing Technology
激光加工技术

1. Introduction 简介

1.1 What is laser? 激光是什么

The word laser is an acronym that stands for "light amplification by stimulated emission of radiation". In a fairly unsophisticated sense, a laser is nothing more than a special flashlight. Energy goes in, usually in the form of electricity, and light comes out. But the light emitted from a laser differs from that from a flashlight, and the differences are worth discussing.

You might think that the biggest difference is that lasers are more powerful than flashlights, but this conception is more often wrong than right. True, some lasers are enormously powerful, but many are much weaker than even the smallest flashlight. So power alone is not a distinguishing characteristic of laser light. Actually, there are three differences between light from a laser and light from a flashlight. First, the laser beam is much narrower than a flashlight beam. Second, the white light of a flashlight beam contains many different colors of light, while the beam from a laser contains only one, pure color. Third, all the light waves in a laser beam are aligned with each other, while the light waves from a flashlight are arranged randomly.

Lasers come in all sizes – from tiny diode lasers small enough to fit in the eye of a needle to huge military and research lasers that fill a three-story building. And different lasers can produce many different colors of light which depend on the length of its waves. Listed in Table 2.1 are some of the important commercial lasers. In addition to these fixed-wavelength lasers, tunable lasers and semiconductor lasers are also commercially available.

Table 2.1 Fixed-wavelength commercial lasers

Laser 激光	Wavelength 波长	Average Power Range 平均功率范围
Carbon dioxide (CO$_2$) 二氧化碳	10.6μm	Milliwatts 毫瓦 to tens of kilowatts
Nd:YAG 钕：石榴石	1.06μm	Milliwatts to hundreds of watts
Nd:glass 钕：玻璃	1.06μm	Pulsed only
Cr:ruby 铬：红宝石	694.3nm (visible)	Pulsed only
Helium-neon 氦氖	632.8nm (visible)	Microwatts 微瓦 to tens of milliwatts
Argon-ion 氩离子	514.5nm (visible)	Milliwatts to tens of watts
	488.0nm (visible)	Milliwatts to watts
Krypton-fluoride 氪氟	248.0nm	Milliwatts to a hundred watts

The "light" produced by carbon dioxide lasers and neodymium lasers cannot be seen by the human eye because it is in the infrared portion of the spectrum. Red light from a ruby or helium-neon laser, and green and blue light from an argon laser, can be seen by the human eye. But the krypton-fluoride laser's output at 248nm is in the ultraviolet range and cannot be directly detected visually.

Interestingly, few of these lasers produce even as much power as an ordinary 100W light bulb. What's more, lasers are not even very efficient. To produce 1W of light, most of the lasers listed in Table 1 would require hundreds or thousands of watts of electricity. What makes lasers worthwhile for many applications, however, is the narrow beam they produce. Even a fraction of a watt, crammed into a super narrow beam, can do things no light bulb could ever do.

Table 2.1 is by no means a complete list of the types of lasers available today, indeed, a complete list would have dozens, if not hundreds, of entries. It is also incomplete in the sense that many lasers can produce more than a single, pure color. Nd:YAG lasers, for example, are best known for their strong line at 1.06μm, but these lasers can also lase at dozens of other wavelengths. In addition, most helium-neon lasers produce red light, but there are other helium-neon lasers that produce green light, yellow light, or orange light, or infrared radiation. Also obviously missing from Table 2.1 are semiconductor diode lasers, with outputs as high as 1W in the near infrared portion of the spectrum, and dye lasers with outputs up to several tens of watts in the visible.

The ruby, yttrium aluminum garnet (YAG), and glass lasers listed are solid-state lasers. The light is generated in a solid, crystalline rod that looks much like a cocktail swizzle stick. All the other lasers listed are gas lasers, which generate light in a gaseous medium like a neon sign. If there are solid state lasers and gaseous lasers, it's logical to ask if there's such a thing as a liquid laser. The answer is yes. The most common example is the organic dye laser, in which dye dissolved in a liquid produces the laser light.

1.2 What can lasers do? 激光能做什么

We've seen that lasers usually don't produce a lot of power. By comparison, an ordinary 1200W electric hair dryer is more powerful than 99% of the lasers in the world today. And we've seen that lasers don't even produce power very efficiently, usually wasting at least 99% of the electricity they consume. So what is all the excitement about? What makes lasers so special, and what are they really used for?

The unique characteristics of laser light are what make lasers so special. The capability to produce a narrow beam doesn't sound very exciting, but it is the critical factor in most laser applications. Because a laser beam is so narrow, it can read the minute, encoded information on a stereo CD – or on the barcode patterns in a grocery store. Because a laser beam is so narrow, the comparatively modest power of a 200W carbon dioxide laser can be focused to an intensity that can cut or weld metal. Because a laser beam is so narrow that can create tiny and wonderfully precise patterns in a laser printer. The other characteristics of laser light – its spectral purity and the way its waves are aligned – are also important for some applications. And, strictly speaking, the narrow beam couldn't exist if the light didn't also have the other two characteristics. But from a simple-minded, applications-oriented viewpoint, a laser can be thought of as nothing more than a flashlight that produces a very narrow beam of light.

One of the leading laser applications is materials processing, in which lasers are used to cut, drill, weld, heat-treat, and otherwise alter both metals and nonmetals. Lasers can drill tiny holes in turbine blades more quickly and less expensively than mechanical drills. Lasers have several advantages over conventional techniques of cutting materials. For one thing, unlike saw blades or knife blades, lasers never get dull. For another, lasers make cuts with better edge quality than most mechanical cutters. The edges of metal parts cut by laser rarely need be filed or polished because the laser makes such a clean cut.

Laser welding can often be more precise and less expensive than conventional welding techniques. Moreover, laser welding is more compatible with robotics, and several large machine-tool builders offer fully automated laser welding systems to manufacturers.

Laser heat-treating involves heating a metal part with laser light, increasing its temperature to the point where its crystal structure changes. It is often possible to harden the surface in this manner, making it more resistant to wear. Heat-treating requires some of the most powerful industrial lasers, and it's one application in which the raw power of the laser is more important than the narrow beam. Although heat-treating is not a wide application of lasers now, it is one that is likely to expand significantly in coming years.

One of the more exciting applications of lasers is in the field of telecommunications, in which tiny diode lasers generate the optical signal transmitted through optical fibers. Because the bandwidth of these fiber optic systems is so much greater than that of conventional copper wires, fiberoptics is playing a major role in enabling the fast-growing Internet.

Modern fiberoptic telecommunication systems transmit multiple wavelengths through a single fiber, a technique called wavelength division multiplexing. The evolution of this technology, together with erbium-doped fiber amplifiers to boost the signal at strategic points along the transmission line, is a major driving force in today's optoelectronics market.

Lasers started out in research laboratories, and many of the most sophisticated ones are still being used there. Chemists, biologists, spectroscopists, and other scientists count lasers among the most powerful investigational tools of modern science. Again, the laser's narrow beam is valuable, but in the laboratory the other characteristics of laser light are often important too. Because a laser's beam contains light of such pure color, it can probe the dynamics of a chemical reaction while it happens or it can even stimulate a reaction to happen.

In medicine, the laser's narrow beam has proven a powerful tool for therapy. In particular, the carbon dioxide laser has been widely adopted by surgeons as a bloodless scalpel because the beam cauterizes an incision even as it is made. Indeed, some surgeries that cause profuse bleeding have been impossible to perform before the advent of the laser. The laser is especially useful in ophthalmic surgery because the beam can pass through the pupil of the eye and weld cut or cauterize tissue inside the eye. Before lasers, any procedure inside the eye necessitated cutting open the eyeball.

Laser printers are capable of producing high-quality output at very high speeds. Until a decade ago, they were also very expensive, but good, PC-compatible laser printers can now be obtained for a few hundred dollars. In a laser printer, the laser "writes" on an electrostatic surface, which, in turn, transfers toner to the paper.

Lasers have other applications in graphics as well. Laser typesetters write directly on light-sensitive paper, producing camera-ready copy for the publishing industry. Laser color separators analyze a color photograph and create the information a printer needs to print the photograph with four colors of ink. Laser platemakers produce the printing plates, or negatives in some cases, so that newspapers such as the Wall Street Journal and USA Today can be printed in locations far from their editorial offices.

And everyone has seen the laser bar-code scanners at the checkout stand of the local grocery store. The narrow beam of the laser in these machines scans the bar-code pattern, automatically reading it into the store's computer.

So far lasers have been found to make weapons, and many scientists believe that engineering complexities and the laws of physics may prevent them from ever being particularly useful for this purpose. Nonetheless, many thousands of lasers have found military applications not in weapons but in range finders and target designators.

A laser range finder measures the time of a pulse of light, usually from an Nd:YAG laser, takes to travel from the range finder to the target and back. An on-board computer divides this number into the speed of light to find the range to the target. A target designator illuminates the target with laser light, usually infrared light from an Nd:YAG laser. Then a piece of "smart" ordnance, a rocket or bomb, equipped with an infrared sensor and some steering mechanism aims the target and destroys it.

Diode lasers are sometimes used to assist in aiming small objects. The laser beam is prealigned along the trajectory of the bullet, and a policeman or soldier can see where the bullet will hit before he fires. Diode lasers are used as military training devices in a scheme that has been mimicked by civilian toy manufacturers. Trainees use rifles that fire bursts of diode-laser light (rather than bullets) and wear an array of optical detectors that score a hit when an opponent fires at them.

There seems to be no end to the ingenious ways a narrow beam of light can be put to use. In sawmills, lasers are used to align logs relative to the saw. The laser projects a visible stripe on the log to show where the saw will cut it as the sawman moves the log into the correct position. On construction projects the narrow beam from a laser guides heavy earth-moving equipment. And laser gyroscopes guide the newest generation of commercial aircraft.

2. Material Laser Processing 材料激光加工

Laser processing is difficult to control because of the nature and complexity of the phenomena and processes. In addition, as the majority of the technological systems, laser systems are complex (depending on many and very different influencing factors), diffuse (with significant interactions between the involved factors) and weakly arranged (having, at least, a partial stochastic behavior).

2.1 Laser bending 激光折弯

Laser bending is a newly developed flexible technique capable of modifying the curvature of sheet metal by thermal residual stresses without any externally applied mechanical forces. Laser bending may also serve the purpose of straightening thin sheets by a similar laser based non-contact process without mechanical forces. The process assumes significance due to the ease and flexibility of non-contact processing, amenability to materials with diverse shape, properties and chemistry, and high precision/productivity. Laser bending involves a complex interplay between the thermal profile generated by the laser irradiation and physical properties of the material/work-piece. The dimensional accuracy of parts produced by bending processes is a topical issue. In general, the process is influenced by many parameters such as laser parameters (power density and interaction/pulse time), material properties (thermal conductivity, coefficient of thermal expansion, etc.) and target dimensions (thickness, curvature, etc.). Laser bending of high strength alloys has been an important motivation for the increasing interest in laser forming process. However, success in laser bending of thick > 1–2mm/ high strength steel or superalloy sheets is not yet achieved. The materials mostly amenable to bending are Al/Ti-alloys and stainless or low alloy steels. Apart from metallic sheets, the success of laser bending of semiconductor and polymeric sheets are eagerly awaited by the semiconductor and packaging industry.

Laser bending is possible only above a threshold heat input. With sufficient thermal input, bending angle decreases significantly with increasing material thickness. However, bending angle no longer increases with increasing heat input beyond an upper critical value of energy input. The decreasing bend rate with increasing irradiation over the same track may be attributed to increase in elastic modulus due to the thickening of the material along the bending edge. A two-dimensional plane strain numerical analysis to calculate the bending angle in pulsed laser irradiation of stainless steel sheet has shown that both optical reflectivity and thermal expansion coefficient constitute the most important considerations that influence the precision of the predicted bending angle. However, suitable correlation between bending dimension and laser parameters would require proper estimation of the effect of relevant material properties at high temperature on the laser bending.

2.2 Laser rapid prototyping 激光快速成型

One of the most recent applications of laser in material processing is development of rapid prototyping technologies, where, lasers have been coupled with computer controlled positioning stages and computer aided engineering design to enable new capability. This development implies that manufacturers are no longer constrained to shape metals by removal of unwanted material. Instead, components can now be shaped into near-net shape parts by addition-building the object in lines or layers one after another. Rapid prototyping relies on "slicing" a 3-dimensional computer model to get a series of cross-sections that can then be made individually. The major techniques for making the slices are stereolithography, selective laser sintering, laminated object manufacturing and fused deposition modelling.

Fig. 2.1 (a) and (b) schematically show basic processes involved in stereolithography and selected laser sintering processes, respectively. In stereolithography, the solid object is made by scanning an ultraviolet (UV) laser beam over the surface of epoxy resin that hardens on exposure to the UV light (Fig. 2.1(a)). Once a layer is complete, the base plate moves down a little in the bath, and a new layer of liquid flows in over the top to enable the next layer to form on top. The layer building continues until the component is ready in the desired dimension. In selective laser sintering, instead of liquid resin, a fluidized powder bed or sheet is used that is heated to close to its melting point (Fig. 2.1(b)). The carbon dioxide laser beam scans over the powder and heats the grains so that they undergo incipient skin melting and sinter. Subsequently, the base plate moves down slightly, and the next layer of powder is spread across the surface by a rotating roller. The process continues until the desired shape or object is ready.

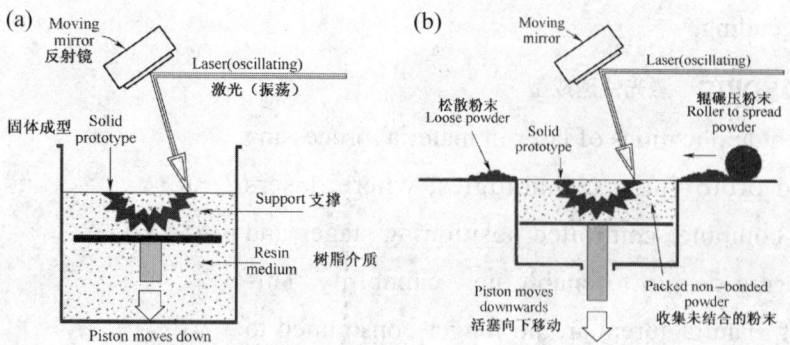

Fig. 2.1 Schematic set-up for laser rapid prototyping by
(a) stereolithography and (b) selected laser sintering

Fig. 2.1(a) and (b) present the scheme of laminated object manufacturing and fused deposition process of prototyping, respectively. In laminated object manufacturing, the preform is built from the layers by pulling long and thin sheets of pre-glued paper/plastic across the base plate and fixing it in place with a heated roller that activates the glue (Fig. 2.2(a)). A computer controlled laser head scans the surface and cuts out the outline of the desired object. As the base plate moves down, the whole process starts again. At the end of the build process, the little crosshatched columns are broken away to free the object. In fused deposition process, the object is made by squeezing a continuous thread of the material through a narrow nozzle (heated by laser) that is moved over the base plate (Fig. 2.2(b)). As the thread passes through the nozzle, it melts only to harden again immediately as it touches the layer below. For certain shapes, a support structure is needed, and this is provided by a second nozzle squeezing out a similar thread, usually of a different colour to make separating the two easier. At the end of the build process, the support structure is broken away and discarded, freeing the object/model. The models made from wax or plastics in this method are physically robust. This new fabrication concept allows construction of complex parts, starting from a 3D–CAD model without a mould.

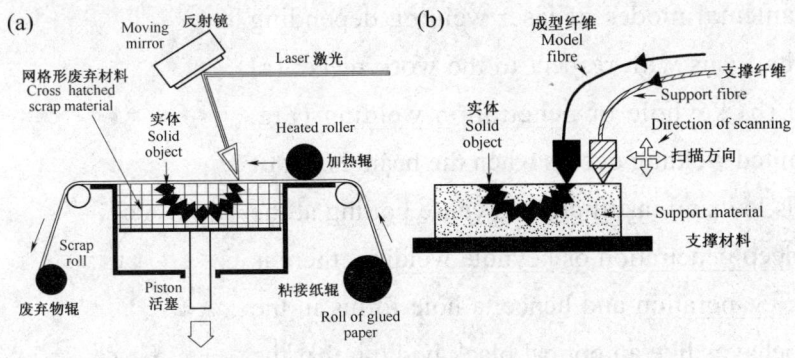

Fig. 2.2 Schematic set-up for laser rapid prototyping by
(a) laminated object manufacturing and (b) fused laser deposition technique

激光快速成型原理图
(a) 分层实体制造
(b) 熔融激光沉积

2.3 Laser welding 激光焊接

Laser welding, because of the sheer proportion of work and advancement over the years, constitutes the most important operations among the laser joining processes. Fig. 2.3 shows the view of the schematic set-up for laser welding without a filler rod. The focused laser beam is made to irradiate the work piece or joint at the given level and speed. A shroud gas protects the weld pool from undue oxidation and provides with the required oxygen flow. Laser heating fuses the work piece or plate edges and joins once the beam is withdrawn. In case of welding with filler, melting is primarily confined to the feeding wire tip while a part of the substrate being irradiated melts to insure a smooth joint. In either case, the work piece rather than the beam travels at a rate conducive for welding and maintaining a minimum heat affected zone.

绝对
进步 / 构成
连接工艺 / 原理示意图
焊条
照射
笼罩 / 过度氧化
氧气流
连接处 / 光束
撤销 / 填充 / 限制
进线端 / 基材
有益的 / 维护
热影响区

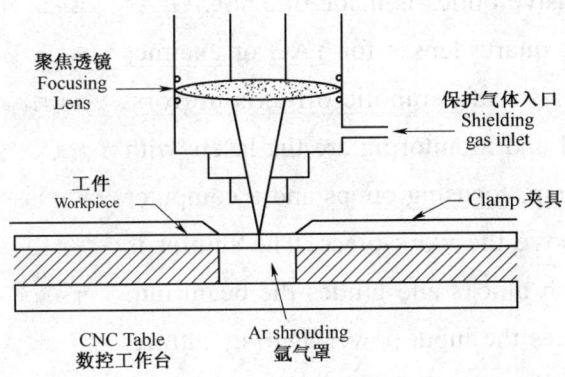

Fig. 2.3 Schematic of laser welding

激光焊接示意图

There are two fundamental modes of laser welding depending on the beam power and its focus with respect to the work piece: (a) conduction welding and (b) keyhole or penetration welding (Fig. 2.4(a)(b)). Conduction limited welding occurs when the beam is out of focus and power density is low and insufficient to cause boiling at the given welding speed. In deep penetration or keyhole welding, there is sufficient energy to cause evaporation and hence, a hole forms in the melt pool. The 'keyhole' behaves like an optical black body in that the radiation enters the hole and is subjected to multiple reflections before being able to escape. The transition from conduction mode to deep penetration mode occurs with increase in laser intensity and duration of laser pulse applied to the work piece.

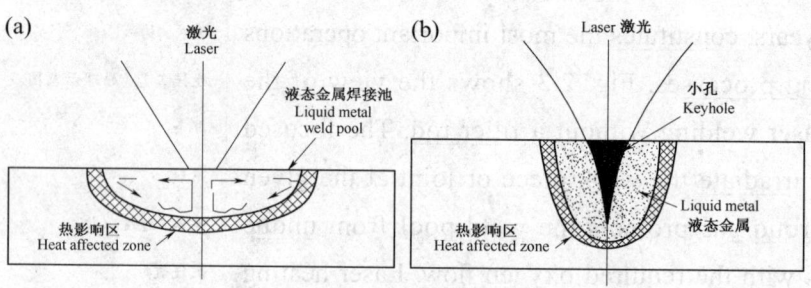

Fig. 2.4 Schematic view of
(a) conduction melt pool and (b) deep-penetration (keyhole) welding

2.4 Laser cutting 激光切割

The general arrangement for cutting with a laser is shown in Fig. 2.5 (a) and (b). The cutting is done either using a transmissive or reflecting optics. The transmissive optics is made of ZnSe, GaAs or CdTe lenses for CO_2 lasers or quartz lenses for YAG or excimer lasers. The reflective optics consists of parabolic off-axis mirrors. The main constituents for control and monitoring are the lasers with shutter control, beam guidance train, focusing optics and a computer controlled translation stage to move the work-piece. The shutter is usually a retractable mirror, which blocks and guides the beam into a water-cooled device that measures the input power. During cutting, the mirror rapidly moves out and allows the beam to be directed on to the work piece after passing through the beam guide that directs the beam to center on a focussing optic. The focussed beam then passes through a nozzle from which a coaxial jet flows. The gas jet is needed both to aid the cutting operation and to protect the optics from spatter. For cutting processes, which rely on melt removal by the gas jet, there is a problem for the metal optics system. To achieve a gas jet suitable for cutting (>20 m/s and reasonably well focussed) without interposing a transmissive elements, a set of centrally directed nozzles or a ring jet can be used. For cutting non-conducting materials like wood, carbon and plastics, the focussed beam heats up the surface to boiling point and generates a keyhole. The keyhole causes a sudden increase in absorptivity due to multiple reflections and the hole deepens quickly. The parameters controlling the laser cutting operation are beam diameter, laser power, traverse speed, gas composition, material thickness, reflectivity and thermo-physical properties.

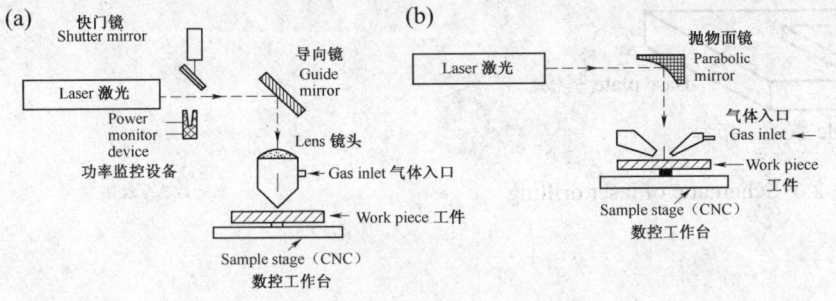

Fig. 2.5 Schematic of laser cutting using
(a) transmissive optics and (b) reflective optics

2.5 Laser drilling 激光钻孔

High power CO_2 lasers or Nd:YAG lasers may also be used to drill holes. Fig. 2.6 shows the basic set used in laser drilling, which is not very different from that used for other laser machining processes. Laser drilling can be done in both pulse and continuous wave modes with suitable laser parameters. The advantage of the laser is that it can drill holes at an angle to the surface. Mechanical drilling is slow and causes extrusions at both ends of the hole that have to be cleaned. Mechanical punching is fast but is limited to holes further than 3mm diameter. Electro chemical machining is too slow at 180s/hole but does give a neat hole. Electro discharge machining is expensive and slow at 58s/hole. Electron beam drilling is fast at 0.125s/hole but needs a vacuum chamber and is more expensive than a YAG laser processing. In comparison, a YAG laser takes 4s/hole to outsmart all other methods.

电火花加工
电子束钻孔
真空室
优于

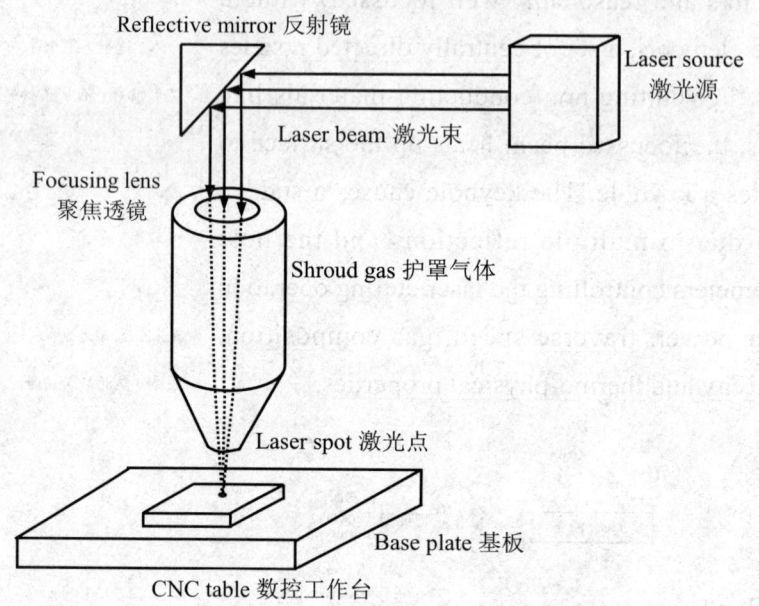

Fig. 2.6 Schematic of laser drilling 激光钻孔原理图

专业词汇

laser beam 激光束
carbon dioxide 二氧化碳
infrared 红外线
spectrum 光谱
ruby 红宝石
ultraviolet(UV) 紫外线
semiconductor diode 半导体二极管
solid-state 固态
crystalline rod 晶棒
gaseous medium 气体介质
organic dye laser 有机染料激光
barcode pattern 条码图案
intensity 强度

coefficient of thermal expansion 热膨胀系数
curvature 曲率
alloy 合金
laser forming process 激光成形工艺
stainless steel sheet 不锈钢板
elastic modulus 弹性模量
plane strain 平面应变
optical reflectivity 光学反射率
rapid prototyping 快速原型
slicing 切片
cross-section 横截面
stereolithography 光固化
selective laser sintering 选择性激光烧结

weld 焊接
drill 钻孔
heat-treat 热处理
manufacturer 制造商
crystal 晶体
resistant to wear 耐磨损
optical fiber 光导纤维
fiberoptic 光纤
dynamics 动力学
typesetter 排版
platemaker 制版机
laser bending 激光折弯
residual stress 残余应力
thin sheet 薄板
productivity 生产率
amenability 屈服
dimensional accuracy 尺寸精度
irradiation 辐射
thermal conductivity 导热系数
mould 铸模
filler rod 焊条

laminated object manufacturing 分层实体制造
fused deposition modelling 熔融沉积成型
epoxy resin 环氧树脂
exposure 曝光
melting point 熔点
sinter 烧结
nozzle 喷嘴
surgery 外科手术
oxidation 氧化
deep penetration welding 深熔焊
keyhole welding 穿透焊
transmissive optics 透射光学系统
reflective optics 反射光学系统
focusing optics 聚焦光学系统
non-conducting material 不导热材料
boiling point 沸点
absorptivity 吸收率
punching 打孔
Electro chemical machining 电化学加工
Electro discharge machining 电火花加工
Electron beam drilling 电子束钻孔

思考题：

1. 激光分为哪几种类型？请简述它们的特点。
2. 请简述激光的用途。
3. 激光快速成型分为哪四种类型？分别描述其工作原理。
4. 激光切割加工需要哪些控制参数？
5. 激光钻孔与其他钻孔方式相比有何优点？

Chapter 3 3D Printing
3D 打印技术

1. Introduction to 3D Printing 3D 打印简介

  3D printing is a form of additive manufacturing technology where a three dimensional object is created by laying down successive layers of material. It is also known as rapid prototyping, is a mechanized method whereby 3D objects are quickly made on a reasonably sized machine connected to a computer containing blueprints for the object. The 3D printing concept of custom manufacturing is exciting to nearly everyone. This revolutionary method for creating 3D models with the use of inkjet technology saves time and cost by eliminating the need to design; print and glue together separate model parts. Now, you can create a complete model in a single process using 3D printing. The basic principles include materials cartridges, flexibility of output, and translation of code into a visible pattern.

  3D Printers are machines that produce physical 3D models from digital data by printing layer by layer (see Fig. 3.1). It can make physical models of objects either designed with a CAD program or scanned with a 3D scanner. It is used in a variety of industries including jewelry, footwear, industrial design, architecture, engineering and construction, automotive, aerospace, dental and medical industries, education and consumer products. The model to be manufactured is built up a layer at a time. A layer of powder is automatically deposited in the model tray. The print head then applies resin in the shape of the model. The layer dries solid almost immediately. The model tray then moves down the distance of a layer and another layer of power is deposited in position, in the model tray. The print head again applies resin in the shape of the model, binding it to the first layer. This sequence occurs one layer at a time until the model is complete (see Fig. 3.2).

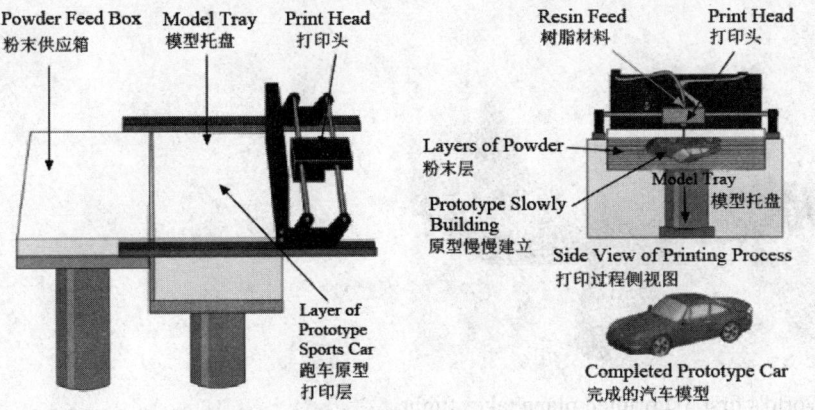

Fig. 3.1 Schematic view of 3D Printers 3D 打印机的组成

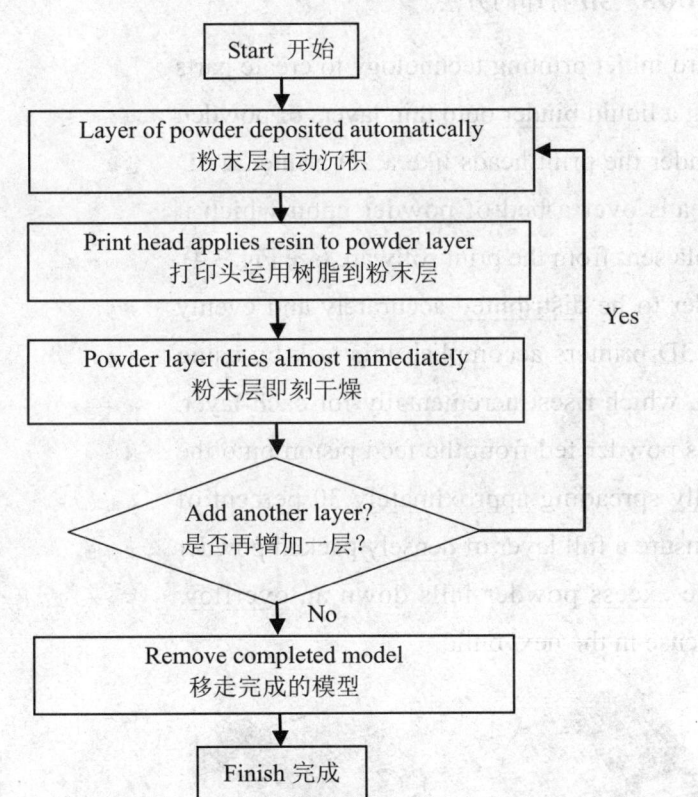

Fig. 3.2 A flow of 3D printing 3D 打印流程

Very recently engineers at the University of Southampton in the UK have designed, printed, and sent skyward, the world's first <u>aircraft</u> manufactured almost entirely via 3-D printing technology(see Fig. 3.3). This aircraft is powered by an electric motor that is pretty much the only part of the aircraft not created via additive manufacturing

航空器

methods.

Fig. 3.3 World's first 3D printed plane takes flight

2. 3D Printing Methods 3D 打印的方法

3D printers use standard inkjet printing technology to create parts layer-by-layer by depositing a liquid binder onto thin layers of powder. Instead of feeding paper under the print heads like a 2D printer, a 3D printer moves the print heads over a bed of powder upon which it prints the cross-sectional data sent from the print software (see Fig. 3.4). The system requires powder to be distributed accurately and evenly across the build platform. 3D printers accomplish this task by using a feed piston and platform, which rises incrementally for each layer. A roller mechanism spreads powder fed from the feed piston onto the build platform; intentionally spreading approximately 30 percent of extra powder per layer to ensure a full layer of densely packed powder on the build platform. The excess powder falls down an overflow chute, into a container for reuse in the next build.

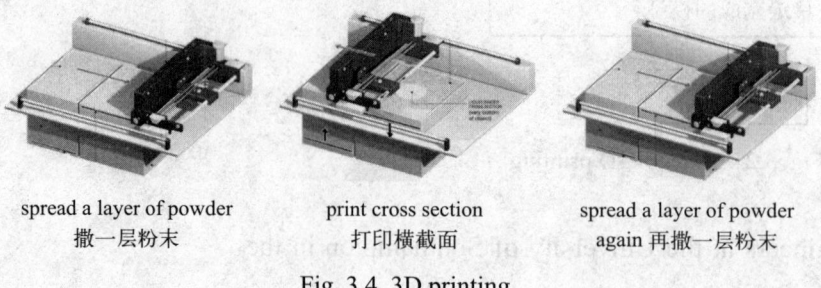

spread a layer of powder 撒一层粉末　　print cross section 打印横截面　　spread a layer of powder again 再撒一层粉末

Fig. 3.4 3D printing

Once the layer of powder is spread, the inkjet print heads print the cross-sectional area for the first, or bottom slice of the part onto the smooth layer of powder, binding the powder together. A piston then lowers the build platform 0.1016mm, and a new layer of powder is spread on top. The print heads apply the data for the next cross section onto the new layer, which binds itself to the previous layer. Print repeats this process for all of the layers of the part. The 3D printing process creates an exact physical model of the geometry represented by 3D data. Process time depends on the height of the part being built. Typically, 3D printers build at a vertical rate of 25mm – 50mm per hour.

When the 3D printing process completes, loose powder surrounds and supports the part in the build chamber. Users can remove the part from the build chamber after the materials have had time to set, and return unprinted, loose powder back to the feed platform for reuse. Users then use forced air to blow the excess powder off the printed part, a short process which takes less than 10 minutes. This technology does not require the use of solid or attached supports during the printing process, and all unused material is reusable.

3. 3D Printers Produce Color Models 3D打印机生产彩色模型

It applies 2D color inkjet methodology to 3D printing and produces the only 3D printers with 24-bit, full-color capabilities. When printing 2D images from digital files, computers convert the RGB values (Red, Green, and Blue colors displayed on the monitor) to CMYK colors (Cyan, Magenta, Yellow, and Black). Typically, a 2D color desktop printer will have a print head with three of the color channels, CMY, and another for black, K. Using these four inks, the printer combines several dots in each printed pixel though the use of dither patterns to create the appearance of thousands of colors. The same principle applies to 3D printing. 3D printers use four colored binders: cyan, magenta, yellow and black, to print colors onto the shell of the part. Print software communicates color information to the printer within the slice data. Full-color 3D printing produces prototypes with the same coloring as the actual product (see Fig. 3.5). Users also use color to represent analysis results directly on the model or to annotate and label design changes to further enhance the communication value of the model. While color can be an <u>essential</u> communications tool, many 3D software packages do not provide a simple way to produce 3D files that include color data.

必不可少

Color prototype shoe　　　　Bottle　　　　Map
彩色鞋子　　　　　　　　彩色瓶子　　　　彩色地图

Fig. 3.5 3D Printers Produce Color Models

3D 打印机打印的彩色模型

专业词汇

additive manufacturing 增材制造
blueprints 设计蓝图
automotive 汽车
aerospace 航空航天
aircraft 航空器
dental 牙科
powder 粉末
automatically 自动地
deposite 堆积

tray 托盘
resin 树脂
binder 粘合剂
platform 平台
mechanism 机构
slice 薄片
forced air 压缩空气
methodology 方法论

思考题：

1. 3D 打印机由哪几部分组成？每部分各有何作用？
2. 描述 3D 打印的一般过程和打印方法。
3. 3D 彩色打印的粘合剂与普通 3D 打印相比有何不同？

Chapter 4   Nanofabrication Technology
纳米加工技术

1. Introduction   介绍

The fabrication of nanostructure is challenging, therefore, a good method for generating nanostructures should enable simultaneous control of the dimensions, properties, and morphology. In general, nanostructures are fabricated/synthesized by promoting the crystallization of solid-state structures or electrons of conductor along one direction by various mechanisms including optical lithography, electron-beam lithography and etc. But due ease in usage and cost effectiveness, here, we employed conventional photolithography to fabricate all the nanostructures. Conventional lithography, resist trimming technique and spacer patterning lithography were used to fabricate the desirable wire of different nano sizes, in all the techniques, the fabrication process steps of nanowire and nanogap are similar. Each one were precisely aligned with previous requirements such as alignment which confirm with the critical dimensions to achieve successful pattern transfer for the whole device design. For technology of device with nano size, misalignment must be controlled to operate within tolerable error limit or total elimination of misalignment but in most cases, such precision needs automatic alignment systems.

2. Nanofabrication Materials   纳米制造材料

All the fabrication methods used silicon substrate, for isolation purpose, silicon nitride and silicon oxide are used and the process started by preparing silicon substrates, a 4 inch wafer, its size need to be well verified prior to starting the process. Before applying further process onto wafer, some properties like thickness and sheet resistance have been checked. The silicon substrates were cleaned and rinsed with de-ionized water. The proper wet cleaning of substrates were done by using RCA1 to reduce undesirable particles, organic particle, metal ion complex lying on the wafer. The deposition of Si3N4 was done by using plasma-enhanced chemical vapor deposition. Plasma nitrides always contain a large amount of hydrogen which provides the enhancement in electrical conductivity, stability, and mechanical stress of thin layer of wafer.

3. Nanofabrication by Lithography 光刻纳米制造

In this technique, the fabrication started with design, as alignment and exposure are the most critical steps in photolithography process, the resolution requirements and precise alignment are vital, each mask needs to be precisely aligned with original alignment mark. Otherwise, it can not successfully transfer the original pattern to the wafer surface causing device and circuit failure. Precise of pattern transfer means guarantee in high repeatability and reliability, high throughput and low cost of ownership. By improving this resolution and alignment precision the minimum size can be further reduced to 1nm and beyond. The other important aspect of achieving minimum precised size is sensitivity. The photoresist must be very sensitive to the exposure light to achieve reasonable throughput. However, if the sensitivity is too high, other photoresist characteristics can be affected, including the resolution of the design.

A silicon nitride is deposited and silane decomposition on the 4 inch silicon wafer, and polysilicon is then deposited on top of the oxide by silane decomposition. Photoresist is spin coated on the polysilicon film, and it is exposed to UV light through a mask shown in Fig. 4.1 that makes the exposed polymer soluble in basic developer solution. The 1μm wire is dry etch by reactive ion etch to get the pattern of exposed polysilicon with size of 1μm and 900nm on various dies on the wafer using with Cl2 and HBr that remove the polysilicon not covered by the photoresist. The next step is to put 1μm and 900nm polysilicon wire on the wafer to the oxidation furnace followed by a CF4 plasma etch to expose the polysilicon, this process continues until the desired size is obtained.

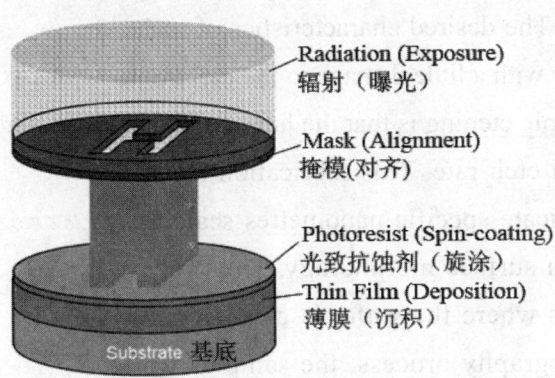

Fig. 4.1 Typical nanofabrication steps with lithography techniques   典型光刻纳米加工步骤

4. Nanogap Fabrication 纳隙加工

A size reduction method was used for the fabrication of the nanogap here. A 100mm p-type silicon wafer is used as a substrate to fabricate the nanogap structure. A mask was designed for the polysilicon nanogap by AutoCAD software. The masks is printed onto a <u>chrome</u> glass surface. We apply <u>dry etching</u> (<u>reactive ion etching</u>, RIE) to <u>pattern</u> the gap (see Fig. 4.2).

铬合金/干刻/活性离子蚀刻
模仿

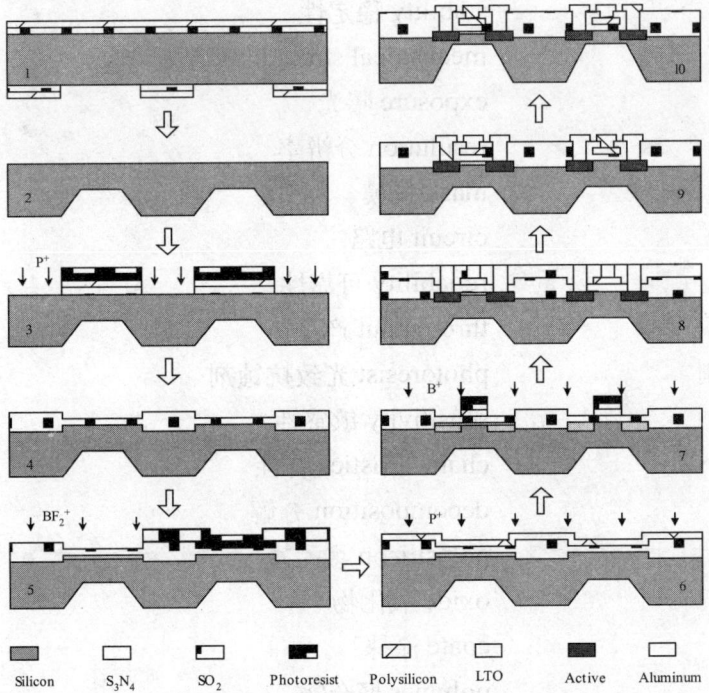

Fig. 4.2 Actual mask and fabrication process of polysilicon nanogap   实际掩模与多晶硅纳米隙加工过程

Size Reduction Lithography(SRL) method of pattern transfer is the selective removal of material. The desired characteristics of such a process include selective anisotropy with a little damage to the electronic device. The consequence of isotropic etching is that the horizontal etch rate is comparable to the vertical etch rate. This fabrication method could potentially be used to fabricate specific nanometres-scale line and space structure with uniform surface morphology. The process started with the cleaning process where the wafer is cleaned using the RCA/BOE. In the photolithography process, the samples were coated with the resist using the spinner. After that, the sample is exposed and aligned using the exposure equipment. Lastly, the ICP-RIE will be used to etch the trimmed resist. After the etching, the samples are inspected under the HPM to see whether the resist is still in good condition or not and observed by profilometer to see the resist been reduced its size.

尺寸减少光刻

可选择地 / 各向异性 / 电子器件

各向同性 / 蚀刻

纳米尺度

形态学

涂抹 / 抗蚀剂 / 旋转机

表面光度仪

专业词汇

nano 纳米
nanostructure 结构
fabrication 加工
dimension 尺寸
property 属性
synthesize 合成
crystallization 结晶
conductor 导体
lithography 光刻
photolithography 照相光刻
nanowire 纳米线
nanogap 纳米间隙
pattern 图案
resist 抗蚀剂
tolerable error 容许误差
silicon 硅
substrate 基底

electrical conductivity 电导率
stability 稳定性
mechanical stress 机械应力
exposure 曝光
resolution 分辨率
mask 掩模
circuit 电路
reliability 可靠性
throughput 产量
photoresist 光致抗蚀剂
sensitivity 敏感性
characteristics 特性
decomposition 分解
polysilicon 多晶硅
oxide 氧化物
coate 涂抹
polymer 聚合物

wafer 晶片
sheet resistance 薄膜电阻
particle 微粒
ion 离子
deposition 沉积
plasma 等离子

etch 蚀刻
die 模子
anisotropy 各向异性
isotropic 各向同性
nanometres-scale 纳米尺度

思考题：

1. 常用的纳米加工方法有哪些？
2. 硅基底材料在进行纳米加工前应如何处理？
3. 描述光刻纳米加工的步骤。
4. 简述使用尺寸减少光刻法进行纳米隙加工的过程。

Chapter 5   Advanced Materials Technology
先进材料技术

1. Hard Coating with Thermal Spraying Processes
热喷涂法硬质涂层

  The earliest records for thermal spraying are patents by the Swiss engineer M. U. Schoop, originating in the early 1900s. At first lead and tin wires were melted in a welding torch by the energy of an acetylene/oxygen flame. The torches then were modified for the use of powdered materials. The wire-arc spraying process was patented around 1908, also by Mr. Schoop, making the deposition of more, and various metals possible. Due to the development of thermal plasmas, and the increasing demand of high temperature and wear resistant materials and coating systems, the thermal spraying technologies expanded in the 70s. Since the 80s the major developments are leading towards increasing particle velocities. Nowadays thermal spraying includes all processes where coating materials are partially, or totally molten, either inside or outside of a spray torch, and the liquid or solid particles are deposited onto a surface, where the arriving droplets form a coating.

  One of the advantages of thermal spraying is the fact that the molten, or partly molten coating material droplets are deposited onto a substrate material without melting it, since only slight heating of the substrate occurs. Therefore, usually no influence on heat treatments, chemical compositions, etc., is observed due to the moderate heat input by thermal spray coating processes, and substrate temperatures seldom exceed 150°C. The tendency of substrate distortion due to substrate heating is considerably lower than for hard facing welding processes (arc, oxy/fuel, electron beam, laser, etc.), where the substrate material is partially molten. This may be the reason for a decrease in certain material properties. However, these fusion processes do have a metallurgical bond, which increases the bond strength to values that thermal spray processes do not achieve.

The coating material may be heated and accelerated through various types of energy release. Fig. 5.1 illustrates the major categories of thermal spray processes.

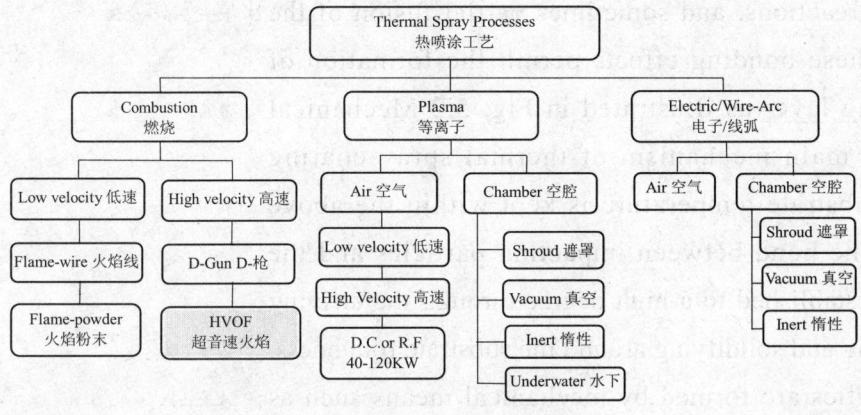

Fig. 5.1 Thermal spray processes

While the particles are accelerated in a gas jet (flame, plasma), they are heated up, and partly or totally molten, depending on their dwell time, which is a function of the average particle size distribution, and temperature distribution within the jet as well. During the flight the particles may interact with the surrounding medium, e.g., oxidation may occur due to their high temperature at their active surface when sprayed in air.

In the electric wire-arc spray process, however, the sprayed materials are wires, which are melted by an electric arc. Therefore, the accelerated droplets are always in a molten state, but their temperature starts to decrease immediately after they are formed from the wire tips. The liquid spray particles form a splat when impacting at the substrate due to their temperature and high kinetic energy, i.e., they are flattened, fractured, spread, and quenched within a very short period of time. Due to the radial spreading, the increase in surface area, and the rather small mass, a rapid quenching of the particles takes place. The necessary time for solidification is between about 10–8 and 10–6 seconds.

2. The Bonding Mechanisms of Thermally Sprayed Coatings 热喷涂的粘接机理

During the rapid solidification of the spray particles there is a close contact between particles and/or the substrate surface. This leads to bonding effects due to mechanical interlocking, adhesion, diffusion, chemical reactions, and sometimes partial fusion of the contact surfaces. These bonding effects permit the formation of a continuous coating layer as illustrated in Fig. 5.2 Mechanical interlocking is the main mechanism of thermal spray coating adherence, if the substrate temperature is kept within the above mentioned range. The bond between impacting particles and the substrate surface is established to a high degree through the arriving droplets liquid flowing and solidifying around the substrate roughness. Usually these asperities are formed by mechanical means such as abrasive blasting, grit blasting, or rough turning, which also activate and clean the surfaces prior to coating. The quenching stresses within the spray particles increase the interlocking effects.

机械互锁 / 粘附
扩散 / 部分熔融
涂层
粘附
液滴 / 粗糙处
表面凸点
喷砂法 / 喷丸 / 粗车 / 激活
冷却应力
互锁效应

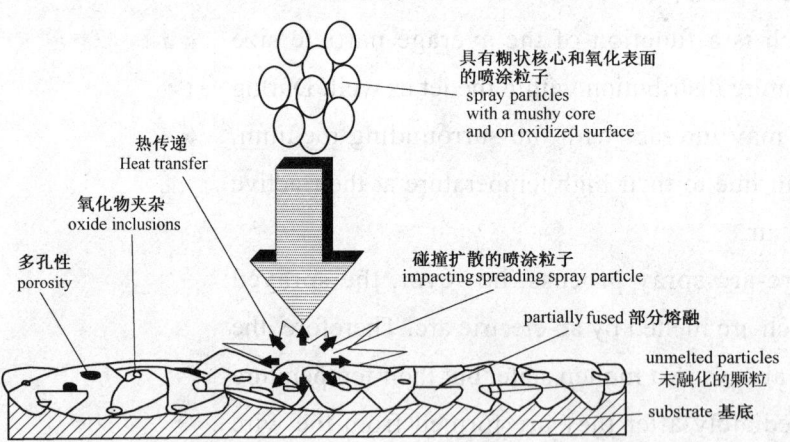

Fig. 5.2 Schematic of a typical structure during thermal spray coating

热喷涂过程中的典型结构示意图

The industrial applications of thermally sprayed coatings largely depend on the bond quality between the coating and substrate. Therefore, a thorough substrate surface preparation is a necessity. Contaminants such as rust, scale, grease, moisture, etc., must be removed from the surface. After cleaning, usually a roughening of the substrate surface follows to ensure coating adhesion. Common

彻底的
污垢物 / 锈 / 屑 / 油脂 / 水分
粗糙化
涂层 / 粘附

methods for surface roughening, which are often combined, are <u>dry abrasive grit blasting</u>, <u>machining roughening</u> and applying a <u>bond coat</u>. The thermal spray coating process should start as soon as possible after the surface preparation is completed, since the prepared surface is very active, and <u>oxidation</u>, <u>recontamination</u>, etc., should be avoided. In some cases, <u>preheating</u> of the substrate materials may be necessary just prior to the coating in order to drive <u>moisture</u> from the substrate. For this purpose substrate preheating in air up to 150°C – 200°C for approximately 60 seconds is sufficient.

干磨料喷砂处理/机械粗加工

粘接涂层

氧化/再污染

预加热

水分

专业词汇

thermal spraying 热喷涂
patent 专利
lead 铅
tin 锡
welding torch 焊枪
acetylene/oxygen flame 氧炔焰
wire-arc spraying 电弧喷涂
wear resistant 耐磨
melt 熔化
droplet 液滴
heat treatment 热处理
distortion 变形
fusion 融合
metallurgical 冶金的

bond 粘合剂
particle 粒子
flame 火焰
oxidation 氧化
splat 喷溅
kinetic energy 动能
quench 冷却
solidification 凝固
adhesion 粘附
diffusion 扩散
adherence 粘附
roughness 粗糙
rust 锈
moisture 水分

思考题：

1. 热喷涂法在材料修复中具有哪些优点？
2. 简述热喷涂方法的粘接机理。
3. 在热喷涂之前需要做哪些准备工作？
4. 热喷涂中常用的表面粗糙化处理方法有哪些？

Part II

Manufacturing Automation Technology

制造自动化技术

Chapter 6　CAD/CAM/CAE/CAPP
计算机辅助设计 / 制造 / 工程 / 工艺规划

1. CAD/CAM/CAPP　计算机辅助设计 / 制造 / 工艺

Throughout the history of our industrial society, many inventions have been patented and whole new technologies have evolved. Perhaps the single development that has impacted manufacturing more quickly and significantly than any previous technology is the digital computer. Computers are being used increasingly for design of engineering components in the drawing office.

Computer aided design (CAD) is defined as the application of computers and graphics software to aid or enhance the product design from conceptualization to documentation. CAD is most commonly associated with the use of an interactive computer graphics system, referred to as a CAD system. Computer-aided design systems are powerful tools and are used in the mechanical design and geometric modeling of products and components. There are several good reasons for using a CAD system to support the engineering design function: (1) To increase the productivity; (2) To improve the quality of the design; (3) To uniform design standards; (4) To create a manufacturing database; (5) To eliminate inaccuracies caused by hand-copying of drawings and inconsistency between drawings.

Models in CAD can be classified as being two-dimensional models, two-and-half-dimensional models, or three-dimensional models. A 2-D model represents a flat part and a 3-D model provides representation of a part shape. A 2.5-D model can be used to represent a part of constant section with no side-wall details. The major advantage of a 2.5-D model is that it gives a certain amount of 3-D information about a part that without the need to create the database of a full 3-D model.

CAM can be defined as computer aided preparation manufacturing including decision-making, process and operational planning, software design techniques, and artificial intelligence, and manufacturing with different types of automation (NC machine, machine center, NC machine cell, flexible manufacturing systems), and different types of realization. The CAM covers group technology, manufacturing database, NC programming and tolerance. When a design has frozen, manufacturing can begin. Computers have an important role to play in many aspects of production. Modern shipbuilding starts from welded steel plates that are cut from a large steel sheet. Computer-controlled flame cutters are often used for this task and the computer is used to calculate the optimum layout of the components to minimize waste metal.

Computer aided process planning (CAPP) can be defined as the functions which use computers to assist the work of process planners. The levels of assistance depend on the different strategies employed to implement the system. Lower level strategies only use computers for storage and retrieval of the data for the process plans which will be constructed manually by process planners, as well as for supplying the data which will be used in the planner' new work. In comparison with lower level strategies, higher level strategies use computers to automatically generate process plans for some workpieces of simple geometrical shapes. Sometimes a process planner is required to input the data needed or to modify plans which do not fit specific production requirements well. The highest level strategy, which is the ultimate goal of CAPP, generates process plans by computer, which may replace process planners, when the knowledge and expertise of process planning and working experience have been incorporated into the computer programs. The database in a CAPP system based on the highest level strategy will be directly integrated with conjunctive systems, e.g. CAD and CAM. CAPP has been recognized as playing a key role in CIMS (Computer integrated manufacturing system).

2. Design Analysis/CAE 设计分析 / 计算机辅助工程

After a particular design alternative has been developed, some form of engineering analysis must often be performed as a part of the design process. The analysis may take the form of stress-strain calculations, heat transfer analysis, dynamic simulation etc. Some examples of the software typically offered on CAD systems are mass properties and Finite Element Method (FEM) analysis. Mass properties involve the computation of such features of a solid object as its volume, surface area, weight, and gravity. FEM analysis is available on most CAD systems to aid in heat transfer, stress-strain analysis, dynamic characteristics, and other engineering computations. Presently, many CAD systems can automatically generate the 2-D or 3-D FEM meshes which are essential to FEM analysis.

The computer has simplified the design analysis stage of the design process significantly. Once a proposed design has been developed, it is necessary to analyze how it will stand up to the conditions to which it will be subjected. Such analysis methods as heat transfer and stress strain calculations are time-consuming and complex. With CAD/CAM, special computer programs written specifically for analysis purposes are available. One such program that has simplified the analysis of manufactured products is called finite-element analysis (FEA). Finite-element analysis involves breaking an object up into many small rectangular or triangular elements (see Fig. 6.1), then analyzing each individual element by computer. This approach gives a thorough analysis that advantage of specifically pinpointing the locations of problem so that design corrections can be more easily made.

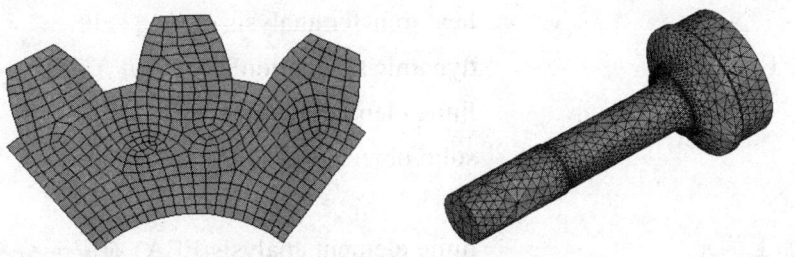

Fig. 6.1 FEA meshes of mechanical parts

With finite-element analysis, the computer must have a powerful processing capability. The computer analyzes the whole object by analyzing each element of the object to the stress, strain, heat, or other force acting on it, the computer can predict the reaction of the whole object. Modern CAD/CAM systems with finite-element analysis capability make the process simple to achieve. Users first define the area that is to be divided and the computers then automatically divides the area into the interconnected network of finite elements. 相互连接 A particularly valuable characteristic of finite-element analysis is its ability to visually display the results of the analysis. For example, if a 可视地 part is to be analyzed to determine how it will behave when subjected 零件 to a specified amount of stress, the computer is able to superimpose 叠加 the image of the stressed. In this way, the resultant distortion can be 结果 / 变形 easily seen. Such visual evidence of the results can make it easier for the designer to pinpoint the necessary design changes. 指出

专业词汇

manufacturing 制造
components 零部件
computer aided design(CAD) 计算机辅助设计
graphics software 绘图软件
interactive 交互的
mechanical design 机械设计
geometric modeling 几何建模
productivity 生产力
three-dimensional model 三维模型
computer aided manufacturing(CAM) 计算机辅助制造
artificial intelligence 人工智能
automation 自动化
NC machine 数控机床
machine center 加工中心
NC machine cell 数控加工单元
NC programming 数控编程
integrate 集成
conjunctive 连接的

interconnect 相互连接
tolerance 公差
shipbuilding 船舶建造
steel plate 钢板
optimum 优化
layout 布局
computer aided process planning (CAPP) 计算机辅助工艺规划
geometrical shape 几何形状
stress-strain calculation 应力应变计算
heat transfer analysis 热传递分析
dynamic simulation 动力学仿真
finite element method(FEM) 有限元法
solid object 实体对象
mesh 网格
finite element analysis(FEA) 有限元分析
distortion 变形
ultimate goal 终极目标

思考题：

1. 使用 CAD 系统进行工程设计的原因是什么？
2. CAM 涵盖哪些方面的技术？
3. CAPP 系统的终极目标是什么？
4. 什么是 CAE？它可以进行哪些方面的分析？
5. FEA 包括哪些方面的内容？它具有什么有价值的特点？

Chapter 7　Modern CNC Machining Technology
现代数控加工技术

1. The emergence and development 数控机床的产生和发展

One of the most <u>fundamental</u> concepts in the area of advanced manufacturing technologies is <u>numerical control(NC)</u>. <u>Prior to</u> the <u>advent</u> of NC, all <u>machine tools</u> were <u>manually</u> operated and controlled. Machine tools, such as <u>milling machines</u>, <u>turning lathe</u> and <u>drill presses</u>, are operated by a <u>skilled machinist</u> who carefully <u>turns</u> the <u>hand wheels</u> and moves the <u>levers</u> to <u>position</u> the workpiece or <u>cutting tool</u> in the proper <u>orientation</u>. It requires a great deal of operator skill and training to produce.

基本的
数控 / 在之前
出现 / 机床 / 手工
铣床 / 车床
钻床 / 技师
转动 / 手轮 / 操纵杆 / 定位
刀具 / 方向

Among the many limitations associated with manual control machine tools, perhaps none is more <u>prominent</u> than the limitation of operator's skills. With manual control, the quality of the <u>product</u> is directly related to and limited to the skills of the operator. Numerical control is developed to overcome the limitation of human operators and it has done so. Numerical control machines are more accurate than manually operated machines, they can produce parts more <u>uniformly</u>, they are faster, and the long – run tooling costs are lower. NC machine tools were developed before the <u>availability</u> of <u>inexpensive</u> <u>computing power</u> and therefore had an electronic control but not a <u>genuine</u> <u>computerized</u> control. The <u>programs</u> were <u>carried</u> by a <u>punched paper tape</u> or by a <u>plastic tape</u> with a series of <u>magnetic dots</u> and the tape was then fed into the machine where the program could be executed. If any changes were needed in the program, a new tape had to be prepared.

突出的
产品

一致地

可用 / 不贵的 / 计算能力
真正的 / 计算机化
程序 / 执行 / 穿孔纸带
塑料带 / 磁点

Today, <u>computer numerical control(CNC)</u> machine tools are widely used in manufacturing enterprises. Computer numerical control is the automated control of machine tools by a computer and computer program. In contrast, today's programs are typically stored on <u>floppy</u>

计算机数控

软盘

or hard disks, and the program can be easily modified directly at the machine's computer (called the controller) or at a PC workstation. The CNC machines still perform essentially the same functions as manually operated machine tools, but movements of the machine tool are controlled electronically rather than by hand. CNC machine tools can produce the same parts over and over again with very little variation. They can run day and night, week after week, without getting tired. These are obvious advantages over manually operated machine tools, which need a great deal of human interaction in order to do anything. This is not to say that manually operated machine tools are obsolete. They are still used extensively for tool and fixture work, maintenance and repair, and small volume production. However, much of the high and medium volume production work is now performed on CNC machine tools.

Machine may be classified according to the number of axes of numerically controlled movements with respect to Cartesian X-Y-Z coordinates. There may be other movement not numerically controlled. A two-axis machine would have the table moved lengthwise and crosswise in a horizontal plane; a three-axis machine would have an additional vertical movement of the spindle, for example, Four-, five-, or six-axis machines provide additional linear or rotary movements.

Research and development adapted to the current complexity of the manufacturing process, with the structure of the closed-loop control system, a new generation of intelligent CNC system has become possible. NC intelligent system will be a new generation of intelligent computer technology, network technology, CAD/CAM, servo control, adaptive control, dynamic data management and dynamic tool compensation, dynamic simulation and other high technology integrated into one of the manufacturing process central control system.

2. CNC Machine Components 数控机床的组成

Host. It is the subject of CNC machine tools, including machine tools, column, spindle, feed mechanism and other mechanical parts. It is used to complete a variety of machining mechanical parts.

CNC equipment. CNC machine tools is the core, including the hardware (printed circuit boards, monitors, keyboard, communication interface, etc.) and the corresponding software for digital input part program, and complete the input information storage, data transformation, interpolation operations and achieve a variety of control functions.

Drive. It is the implementing agencies CNC drive components, including the spindle drive unit, feed unit, spindle motor and feed motor. It is under the control of the NC device electrical or electro-hydraulic servo system to achieve through the spindle and feed drive. When several feed linkage, you can complete the position, line, plane curves and space curves processing.

Assist device. It is the index control machine tools necessary supporting components to ensure the operation of CNC machine tools, such as cooling, chip removal, lubrication, lighting, monitoring. It consists of hydraulic and pneumatic devices, chip equipment, pallet, NC rotary table and CNC dividing head, including tools and monitoring detection devices.

Programming equipment. It can be used to machine the part outside the programming and storage.

3. Machining Centers 加工中心

The machining center has an automatic tool changing facilities, which called tool magazines. There are a number of different types of tool magazines: chain, circular and box. There are two main types of machining centers: the horizontal spindle and the vertical spindle machine.

Horizontal spindle type. The traveling-column type is equipped with one or usually two tables on which the workpiece can be mounted. With this type of machining center, the workpiece can be machined while the operator is loading a new workpiece on the other table. The fixed-column type is equipped with a pallet shuttle. The pallet is a removable table on which the workpiece is mounted. After the workpiece has been machined, the workpiece and pallet are moved to a shuttle which then rotates, bringing a new pallet and workpiece into position for machining.

  Vertical spindle type. The vertical spindle machining center is a saddle-type construction with sliding bed ways which utilizes a sliding vertical head. The main parts of CNC machining centers are the bed, saddle, column, table, servomotors ball screws, spindle, tool changers, and the machine control unit(MCU).   垂直主轴类型 / 马鞍型 / 床身 / 床鞍/伺服马达/滚珠丝杆/换刀装置

  Bed. The bed is usually made of high quality cast iron which provides for a rigid machine capable of performing heavy-duty machining and maintaining high precision, it provides rigid support for all linear axes.   床身/铸铁 / 刚性的/加工/重型

  Saddle. The saddle, which is mounted on the hardened bed ways, provides the machining center with the X-axis linear movement.   床鞍/硬化的/床轨

  Column. The column, which is mounted to the saddle, is designed with high torsional strength to prevent distortion and deflection during machining. The column provides the machining center with the Y-axis linear movement.   立柱 / 扭转强度/变形/偏转

  Table. The table, which is mounted on the bed, provides the machining center with the Z-axis linear movement.   工作台

  Servo system. The servo system, which consists of servo drive motors, ball screws, and position feedback encoders, provides fast, accurate movement and positioning of the XYZ axes slides. The feedback encoders mounted on the ends of the ball screws form a closed-loop system which maintains consistent high positioning repeatability of ±0.003m.   伺服系统 / 位置反馈编码器 / 末端 / 维持/一致的 / 重复定位精度

  Spindle. The spindle, which is programmable in 1r/min increments, has a speed range of from 20 to 6000r/min. The spindle can be of a fixed position type, or can be a tilting spindle which provides for an additional A axis.   主轴/增量 / 倾斜的

  Tool changers. There are basically two types of tool changers, the vertical tool changer and the horizontal tool changer. The tool changer is capable of storing a number of preset tools which can be automatically called by the program. Tool changers are usually bidirectional, which allows for the shortest travel distance to randomly access a tool. The actual tool change time is usually only 3 to 5s.   换刀装置 / 预设 / 调用 / 双向的/移动 / 访问

MCU. The MCU allows the operator to perform a variety of operations such as programming, machining, diagnostics, tool and machine monitoring, etc. MCUs vary according to manufacturers' specifications, new MCUs are becoming more sophisticated, making machine tools more reliable and the entire machining operations less dependent on human skills.

4. Control System 控制系统

4.1 Positioning Control 位置控制

The basis of numerically controlled machining is the programmed movement of the machine slides to the predetermined position. Three basic path control systems are found in general usage. (1) The point-to-point system effectively disregards the path between points. Each axis of motion is controlled independently so that the path steps from the start position to the next position. Because the traverse path is not controlled, point-to-point systems can only be used in NC applications in which a discrete operation, such as drilling a hole, retracting, drilling another hole, occurs at a given stationary location. (2) Straight-cut systems provide a somewhat greater degree of axis coordination than point to-point devices. The straight-cut system has the ability to accurately follow straight paths along each machine axis. (3) Contouring systems are the most versatile and sophisticated NC devices. The contouring controller generates a path between points by interpolating intermediate coordinates. All contouring systems have a linear interpolation capability. Many systems have additional interpolation capabilities, and because the contouring system provides a predictable accurate path between points, any path in space can be traced.

4.2 Drive System 驱动系统

The drive system is comprised of screws and motors that will finally turn the part program into motion. The first component of the typical drive system is a high-precision lead screw called a ball screw. Eliminating backlash in a ball screw is very important for two reasons. First high-precision positioning cannot be achieved if the table is free to move slightly when it is supposed to be stationary. Second, material can be climb-cut safely if the backlash has been eliminated. Climb cutting is usually the most desirable method for machining on a CNC machine tool.

Drive motors are the second specialized component in the drive system. The turning of the motor will turn the ball screw to directly cause the machining table to move. Several types of electric motors are used on CNC control systems, and hydraulic motors are also occasionally used. The simplest type of electric motor used in CNC positioning systems is the stepper motor. A stepper motor rotates a fixed number of degrees when it receives an electrical pulse and then stops until another pulse is received. The stepping characteristic makes stepper motors easy to control. Modern industrial CNC machines seldom use stepper motors, it is more common to use servomotors in CNC systems today. Servomotors operate in a smooth, continuous motion – not like the discrete movements of the stepper motors. This smooth motion leads to highly desirable machining characteristics, but they are also difficult to control.

顺铣/顺铣

电子马达
液压马达

步进电机
电脉冲

伺服电机

4.3 Feedback System 反馈系统

The function of a feedback system is to provide the control with information about the status of the motion control system. The control can compare the desired condition to the actual condition and make corrections. The most obvious information to be fed back to the control on a CNC machine tool is the position of the table and the velocity of the motors. Other information may also be fed back that is not directly related to motion control, such as the temperature of the motor and the load on the spindle – this information protects the machine from damage.

速率

There are two main types of control systems: open-loop and closed-loop. An open-loop system does not have any device to determine if the instructions were carried out. For example, in an open-loop system, the control could give instructions to turn the motor 10 revolutions. However, no information can come back to the control to tell it if it actually turned. All the control knows is that it delivered the

开环
闭环
指令

旋转

instructions. Open-loop control is not used for critical systems, but it is a good choice for inexpensive motion control systems in which accuracy and reliability are not critical. Closed-loop feedback uses external sensors to verify that certain conditions have been met. Of course, positioning and velocity feedback is of primary importance to an accurate CNC system. Feedback is the only way to ensure that the machine is behaving the way the control intended it to behave.

关键

传感器 / 验证

5. Numerical Control Programming 数控编程

5.1 Code List 代码表

Table 7.1 NC Code 数控代码（FANUC 系统）

M CODES	M 代码		
M00	Program stop 程序停止	M05	Spindle stop 主轴停止
M01	Optional stop 任选停止	M06	Tool change 换刀
M02	End of program 程序结束	M08	Flood coolant on 冷却液开
M03	Spindle CW 主轴正转	M09	Coolant off 冷却液关
M04	Spindle CCW 主轴反转	M30	End of tape 程序结束
G CODES	G 代码		
G00	Rapid traverse 快速移动（定位）	G29	Return from reference point 从参考点返回
G01	Linear interpolation CW 直线插补	G40	Cutter compensation-cancel 取消刀具半径补偿
G02	Circular interpolation CW 圆弧插补（顺时针）	G41	Cutter compensation-left 刀具半径左补偿
G03	Circular interpolation CCW 圆弧插补（逆时针）	G42	Cutter compensation-right 刀具半径右补偿
G04	Dwell 暂停	G43	Cutter compensation-Positive 刀具长度正补偿

（续表）

G08	Acceleration 加速	G44	Cutter compensation-negative 刀具长度负补偿
G09	Deceleration 减速	G49	Cutter compensation-cancel 取消刀具长度补偿
G17	X-Y Plane 选择 XY 平面	G80	Fixed-cycle cancel 取消固定循环
G18	Z-X Plane 选择 ZX 平面	G81-89	Fixed cycles 固定循环
G19	Y-Z Plane 选择 Y-Z 平面	G90	Absolute dimension program 绝对尺寸编程
G28	Return to reference point 返回参考点	G91	Incremental dimension program 增量尺寸编程

5.2 An Example: Circular Interpolation 圆弧插补例子

For circular interpolation, the tool destination and the circle center are programmed in one block. G02 is <u>clockwise</u> interpolation, G03 is <u>counterclockwise</u> interpolation. Specify center with I, J, K, which are the <u>incremental</u> distance from the start of the arc. Viewing the start of arc as the origin, I, J, K have positive or negative signs. Fig. 7.1 is a circular interpolation example and its NC code.

顺时钟方向
逆时针方向
增加的

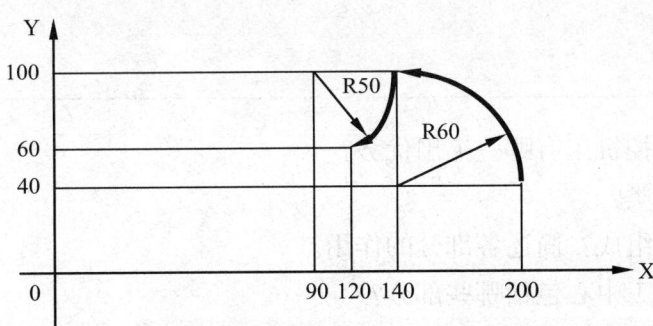

Fig. 7.1 Circular interpolation example

N0010 G92　X200.0　Y40.0　Z0 ;
N0020 G90　G03　X140.0　Y100.0　R-60.0　F300;
N0030 G02　X120.0　Y60.0　R-50.0;
or
N0010 G92　X200.0　Y40.0　Z0;
N0020 G90　G03　X140.0　Y100.0　R60.0　F300;
N0030 G02　X120.0　Y60.0　R50.0;

专业词汇

numerical control(NC) 数控
machine tools 机床
milling machine 铣床
turning lathe 车床
drill presses 钻床
skilled machinist 技师
cutting tool 刀具
computer numerical control(CNC) 计算机数控
small volume production 小批量生产
Cartesian coordinate 笛卡尔坐标
spindle 主轴
manufacturing process 制造工艺
closed-loop 闭环
open-loop 开环
tool compensation 刀具补偿
column 立柱
feed mechanism 进给机构
interpolation 插值
electro-hydraulic servo system 电液伺服系统
lubrication 润滑
hydraulic 液压的

pneumatic 气动的
rotary table 旋转工作台
dividing head 分度头
tool changing 刀具交换
tool magazine 刀库
servomotor 伺服马达
saddle 床鞍
ball screws 滚珠丝杆
cast iron 铸铁
rigid 刚性的
torsional strength 扭转强度
distortion 变形
positioning repeatability 重复定位精度
contouring 轮廓
stepper motor 步进电机
servomotor 伺服电机
coolant 冷却液
cutter compensation 刀具补偿
circular interpolation 圆弧插补
linear interpolation 直线插补

思考题：

1. 与普通机床相比，数控机床有哪些突出优势？
2. 数控机床如何进行分类？
3. 数控机床由哪几部分组成？简述各部分的作用。
4. 什么是加工中心？加工中心包括哪些部分？
5. 数控机床的位置控制方法有哪些？各有何特点？
6. 简述数控机床驱动系统的组成。

Chapter 8   Flexible Manufacturing System
柔性制造系统

1. Introduction   简介

The main advantage of the flexible manufacturing system(FMS) is its high flexibility in management of production facilities and resources (time, machines and their utilization, etc.). The largest application of these systems is in the area of small batch production where its efficiency is getting near to the mass production efficiency. Its disadvantage is the high implementation price.

柔性制造系统
灵活性 / 设备

小批量生产
效率 / 大批量生产
实施

2. Present Situation   现状

At present, industrial production structure and management suitable for large batch production of a narrow product spectrum is predominating. However, such a production structure and management is not satisfactory anymore as the tendency of user individualization manifests. In consequence of small flexibility in responding to market demands, the competitiveness of manufacturers is going down and they are outrun by competitors with an ability to respond to requirements of customers much more flexibly.

大批量生产 / 产品系列
占主导地位
趋势 / 个性化清单

竞争力 / 制造商
超越 / 竞争者

The target to build up a flexible manufacturing system is robotized operation and a drawing-free production. That means, the product will be simulated by PC in a suitable 3-D CAD program, thereafter a control program necessary for production of the component will be generated and this program will be then started up in a flexible manufacturing system that will physically produce that component. In this way it would possible to produce all necessary components for a specific product that will be assembled in the final phase. During production, all components will be subjected to checking operations, consequently, in the final assembly the faulty rate of finished products will be considerably reduced.

自动化作业
无图纸
之后
零件

装配 / 阶段

装配 / 缺陷率

3. Demands on Flexible Manufacturing System
柔性制造系统的需求

A flexible manufacturing system is a group of numerically controlled machine tools, interconnected by a central control system. The various machining cells are interconnected via loading and unloading stations by an automated transport system. Operational flexibility is enhanced by the ability to execute all manufacturing tasks on numerous product designs in small quantities and with faster delivery. It has been described as an automated job shop and as a miniature automated factory. Simply stated, it is an automated production system that produces one or more families of parts in a flexible manner. Today, this prospect of automation and flexibility presents the possibility of producing nonstandard parts to create a competitive advantage.

The concept of flexible manufacturing systems evolved during the 1960s when robots, programmable controllers, and computerized numerical controls brought a controlled environment to the factory in the form of numerically controlled and direct numerically controlled machines.

For the most part, FMS is limited to firms involved in small batch production or job shop environments. Normally, small batch producers have two kinds of equipment from which to choose: dedicated machinery or unautomated, general purpose tools. Dedicated machinery results in cost savings but lacks flexibility. General purpose machines such as lathes, milling machines, or drill presses are all costly, and may not reach full capacity. Flexible manufacturing systems provide the small batch manufacturer with another option one that can make small batch manufacturing just as efficient and productive as mass production.

Flexible manufacturing system with robot operation for environment of drawing-free production will be represented by the model CIM (Computer Integrated Manufacturing). It is a systemic approach to planning, management and production itself. In practice, these experiences, if accepted, can considerably increase competitiveness of industrial companies. Such a competitiveness increase will result from higher efficiency in planning, management and production. Higher efficiency will be seen in shorter production time, higher utilization of machines and tools, higher production flexibility what all together means production cost saving.

The whole FMS must therefore contain a communication structure based on modern industrial standard that is compatible with other industrial facilities to enable trouble-free data transfer. One of marginal conditions for definition of FMS characteristics is the ability to cooperate with CAD system. In addition, this system will also have to cooperate with other CAD software systems. The block diagram of such a modular system is in the Fig. 8.1.

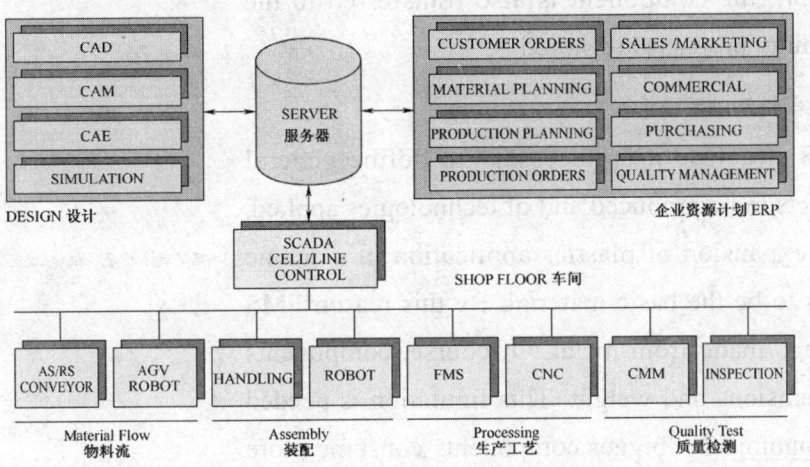

Fig. 8.1 Block diagram of modular flexible manufacturing system

4. FMS Function and Structure 柔性制造系统功能和结构

4.1 FMS Function 功能

FMS can produce various components of shaft, flange, bracket and box shape in this system. Each component made will represent piece production that means only one piece of this component will be made. Variability (dimensions and shape versions for each component) will be relatively wide. Planning and management of the production process in FMS must be adapted to that fact.

The whole process starting with design up to storage of final component must run automatically without human intervention. That means, material in the FMS storage system will be automatically taken out of store, transported to individual machines according to program, put in operating area by a industrial robot. Machine will execute individual technological operations to reach final shape and dimension of the component. Simple components can be worked by one machine only but in case of more complicated parts, the component will have to be handled in other machine or relocated to another machine so that other necessary technological operations can be realized.

After completion of all necessary technological operations the component will be relocated to checking station for quality control and if quality control is successful, the finished and checked component will be automatically transferred to FMS storage system. If the quality control is not successful, the component is also transferred to the storage system where faulty products are stored.

4.2 FMS Structure 柔性制造系统结构

In a term of FMS structure it is necessary to define general characteristics of products to be produced and of technologies applied. In spite of significant expansion of plastics application in machine industry, metal remains to be the basic material. By this reason FMS will produce components made from metal. Of course, components must be limited in dimensions and weight. This limitation is needed by several reasons: Economical – bigger components consume more material, bigger and more expensive machines, higher demands on energy, etc. Spatial – bigger machines require more places. Due to relatively small space available for FMS we must choose to manufacture and handling devices of small dimensions and that means the size of individual components will also be limited.

Technologies that can be used for processing basic metal material into a finished component can be divided as follows. Both metallurgical and mechanical production technologies are energy demanding, cause environmental contamination and require rather big production facilities. This was one of reasons to focus on machining technologies in FMS. Another reason for choice of machining technology for FMS was that more than 80% of all components are machined to their final phase and other technologies actually produce only a suitable semi-product for machining and ultimately are not suitable for piece production.

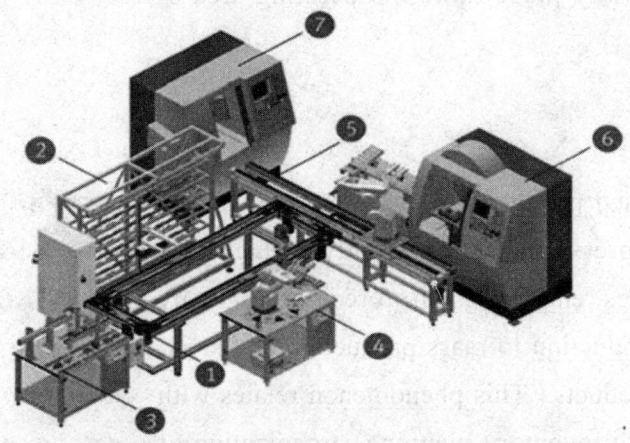

Fig. 8.2 A typical flexible manufacturing system
① conveyor; ② storage; ③ pallet handling and quality station; ④ robot vision and assembly station; ⑤ robot feeder of machine tools; ⑥ CNC lathe; ⑦ CNC milling machine

Fig. 8.2 is the structure of a typical FMS. For production of rotary components, turning operations are used most frequently and milling operations are most frequently used for production of non-rotary components. Accordingly, also FMS will include production facilities that are able to execute these technological operations (lathe and milling machine). As we need a fully automated FMS function, production facilities (machining devices) must be CNC controlled that will enable their integration with other devices of one system. Robotized attendance within FMS will be provided for by industrial robots which will load the semi product into the operating area of individual machining devices or into the operating area of the checking station and unload machined eventually checked components from these devices. FMS must also include an automatic storage facility where various types of semi products as well as finished products will be stored. This storage system must be operated by a feeding device that will take out individual semi products from the storage system and store in finished components. The checking station will check real dimensions and shape of individual components made. This station will also be robotized. All mentioned devices must be linked with the transport system which will ensure transport of semi products and finished components to necessary place to be in operating area of individual industrial robots.

5. Conclusion 总结

Currently, due to shortened product life cycle, market liberalization, a great competitive pressures and constantly dynamically changing demands of customers, enterprises are forced to gradually rebuilding the nature of its production to mass production and small series with a wide range of products. This phenomenon relates with many problems especially with inventory planning, organization of production, rationalization of work. In particular, large enterprises have adapted the nature of their production to mass production, which creates a huge problem with optimization of inventory both in storage and manufacturing, production optimization problems with frequent alterations of machinery and related timing, capacity and economic losses. So designing flexible manufacturing system includes rational and efficient manufacturing and assembly ways and basic intelligence principles.

专业词汇

flexible manufacturing system(FMS) 柔性制造系统
small batch production 小批量生产
mass production 大批量生产
piece production 单件生产
competitiveness 竞争力
manufacturer 制造商
assembly 装配
faulty rate 缺陷率
faulty products 缺陷产品
delivery 交付
direct numerically control(DNC) 直接数控
shaft 轴
environmental contamination 环境污染
industrial robot 工业机器人
feeding device 进料设备
semi product 半成品
rotary component 回转体零件

machining cell 加工单元
lathe 车床
job shop 工作车间
programmable controller 可编程控制器

lathe 车床
conveyor 传送带
product life cycle 产品生命周期
optimization of inventory 库存优化

思考题：

1. 柔性制造系统有何优点？
2. 一个完整的柔性制造系统由哪些模块组成？
3. 典型的柔性制造系统包括哪些设备？各有何作用？

Chapter 9 Computer Integrated Manufacturing System 计算机集成制造系统

1. Introduction 简介

Computer Integrated Manufacturing System(CIMS) encompasses the entire range of product development and manufacturing activities with all the functions being carried out with the help of dedicated software packages. The data required for various functions are passed from one application software to another in a seamless manner. For example, the product data is created during design. This data has to be transferred from the modeling software to manufacturing software without any loss of data. CIM uses a common database where communication technologies to integrate design, manufacturing and associated business functions that combine the automated segments of a factory or a manufacturing facility. CIM reduces the human component of manufacturing and thereby relieves the process of its slow, expensive and error-prone component. CIM stands for a holistic methodological approach to the activities of the manufacturing enterprise in order to achieve vast improvement in its performance.

This methodological approach is applied to all activities from the design of the product to customer support in an integrated way, using various methods, means and techniques in order to achieve production improvement, cost reduction, fulfillment of scheduled delivery dates, quality improvement and total flexibility in the manufacturing system. CIM requires all those associated with a company to involve totally in the process of product development and manufacture. In such a holistic approach, economic, social and human aspects have the same importance as technical aspects.

CIM also encompasses the whole lot of enabling technologies including total quality management, business process reengineering, concurrent engineering, workflow automation, enterprise resource planning and flexible manufacturing.

A distinct feature of manufacturing today is mass customization. This implies that though the products are manufactured in large quantities, products must incorporate customer-specific changes to satisfy the diverse requirements of the customers. This requires extremely high flexibility in the manufacturing system.

Manufacturing industries strive to reduce the cost of the product continuously to remain competitive in the face of global competition. In addition, there is the need to improve the quality and performance levels on a continuing basis. Another important requirement is on time delivery. In the context of global outsourcing and long supply chains cutting across international borders, the task of continuously reducing delivery times is really an arduous task. CIM has several software tools to address the above needs.

Manufacturing engineers are required to achieve the following objectives to be competitive in a global context: reduction in inventory, lower the cost of the product, reduce waste, improve quality, increase flexibility in manufacturing to achieve immediate and rapid response to product changes, production changes, process change, equipment change, change of personnel. CIM technology is an enabling technology to meet the above challenges to the manu-facturing.

The advances in automation have enabled industries to develop islands of automation. Examples are flexible manufacturing cells, robotized work cells, flexible inspection cells etc. One of the objectives of CIM is to achieve the consolidation and integration of these islands of automation. This requires sharing of information among different applications or sections of a factory, accessing incompatible and heterogeneous data and devices. The ultimate objective is to meet the competition by improved customer satisfaction through reduction in cost, improvement in quality and reduction in product development time.

CIM makes full use of the capabilities of the digital computer to improve manufacturing. Two of them are programmable automation and real time optimization. The computer has the capability to accomplish the above for hardware components of manufacturing (the manufacturing machinery and equipment) and software component of manufacturing (the application software, the information flow, database and so on). The capabilities of the computer are thus exploited not only for the various pieces of manufacturing activity but also for the entire system of manufacturing. Computers have the tremendous potential needed to integrate the entire manufacturing system and thereby evolve the computer integrated manufacturing system.

2. Evolution of Computer Integrated Manufacturing
计算机集成制造的演化

Computer Integrated Manufacturing (CIM) is considered a natural evolution of the technology of CAD/CAM which by itself evolved by the integration of CAD and CAM. Massachusetts Institute of Technology (MIT) is credited with pioneering the development in both CAD and CAM. The need to meet the design and manufacturing requirements of aerospace industries after the Second World War necessitated the development these technologies. The manufacturing technology available during late 40's and early 50's could not meet the design and manufacturing challenges arising out of the need to develop sophisticated aircraft and satellite launch vehicles. This prompted the US Air Force to approach MIT to develop suitable control systems, drives and programming techniques for machine tools using electronic control.

The first major innovation in machine control is the Numerical Control (NC) demonstrated at MIT in 1952. Early numerical control systems were all basically hardwired systems, since these were built with discrete systems or with later first generation integrated chips. Early NC machines used paper tape as an input medium. Every NC machine was fitted with a tape reader to read paper tape and transfer the program to the memory of the machine tool block by block. Mainframe computers were used to control a group of NC machines by mid 60's. This arrangement was then called Direct Numerical Control (DNC) as the computer bypassed the tape reader to transfer the program data to the machine controller. By late 60's mini computers were being commonly used to control NC machines. At this stage NC became truly soft wired with the facilities of mass program storage, offline editing and software logic control and processing. This development was called Computer Numerical Control (CNC).

Since 70's, numerical controllers were being designed around microprocessors, resulting in compact CNC systems. A further development to this technology was the distributed numerical control (also called DNC) in which processing of NC program is carried out in different computers operating at different hierarchical levels - typically from mainframe host computers to plant computers to the machine controller. Today the CNC systems are built around powerful 32 bit and 64 bit microprocessors. PC based systems are also becoming increasingly popular.

Manufacturing engineers also started using computers for such tasks like inventory control, demand forecasting, production planning and control etc. CNC technology was adapted in the development of co-ordinate measuring machine's which automated inspection. Robots were introduced to automate several tasks like machine loading, materials handling, welding, painting and assembly. All these developments led to the evolution of flexible manufacturing cells and flexible manufacturing systems in late 70's.

Evolution of Computer Aided Design (CAD), on the other hand was to cater to the geometric modeling needs of automobile and aeronautical industries. The developments in computers, design workstations, graphic cards, display devices and graphic input and output devices during the last ten years have been phenomenal. This coupled with the development of operating system with graphic user interfaces and powerful interactive software packages for modeling, drafting, analysis and optimization provides the necessary tools to automate the design process.

If we review the manufacturing scenario during 80's we will find that the manufacturing is characterized by a few islands of automation. In the case of design, the task is well automated. In the case of manufacture, CNC machines, DNC systems, FMS etc provide tightly controlled automation systems. Similarly computer control has been implemented in several areas like manufacturing resource planning, accounting, sales, marketing and purchase. Yet the full potential of computerization could not be obtained unless all the segments of manufacturing are integrated, permitting the transfer of data across various functional modules. This realization led to the concept of computer integrated manufacturing. Thus the implementation of CIM required the development of whole lot of computer technologies related to hardware and software.

3. CIMS Hardware and Software CIMS 的硬件和软件

CIM Hardware comprises the following: (i) Manufacturing equipment such as CNC machines or computerized work centres, robotic work cells, DNC/FMS systems, work handling and tool handling devices, storage devices, sensors, shop data collection devices, inspection machines etc. (ii) Computers, controllers, CAD/CAM systems, workstations / terminals, data entry terminals, bar code readers , RFID tags, printers, plotters and other peripheral devices, modems, cables, connectors etc.

CIM software comprises computer program to carry out the following functions: Management Information System, Sales, Marketing, Finance, Database Management, Modeling and Design, Analysis, Simulation, Communications, Monitoring, Production Control, Manufacturing Area Control, Job Tracking, Inventory Control, Shop Floor Data Collection, Order Entry, Materials Handling, Device Drivers, Process Planning, Manufacturing Facilities Planning, Work Flow Automation, Business Process Management, Network Management, Quality Management.

4. Major Elements of CIMS CIMS 主要元素

Nine major elements of a CIM system are in Fig. 9.1 They are Marketing, Product Design, Planning, Purchase, Manufacturing Engineering, Factory Automation Hardware, Warehousing, Logistics and Supply Chain Management, Finance, Information Management.

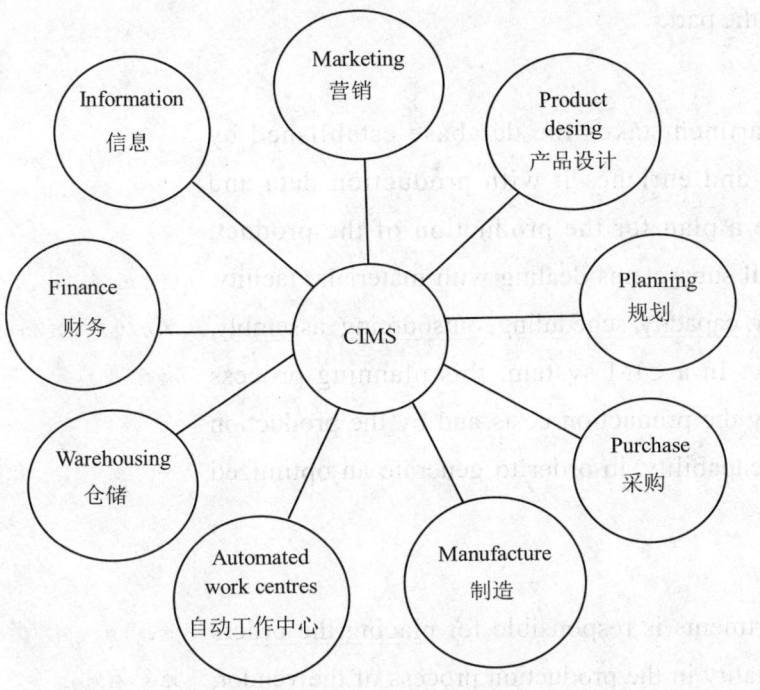

Fig. 9.1 Major Elements of a CIM System

4.1 Marketing　市场营销

The need for a product is identified by the marketing division. The specifications of the product, manufacturing quantities and the strategy for marketing are also decided by the marketing department. Marketing also works out the manufacturing costs to assess the economic viability of the product.

4.2 Product Design　产品设计

The design department of the company establishes the initial database for production of a proposed product. In a CIM system this is accomplished through activities such as geometric modeling and computer aided design while considering the product requirements and concepts generated by the creativity of the design engineer. Configuration management is an important activity in many designs. Complex designs are usually carried out by several teams working simultaneously, which often located in different parts of the world. The design process is constrained by the costs that will be incurred in actual production and by the capabilities of the available production equipment and processes. The design process creates the database required to manufacture the part.

4.3 Planning 计划

The planning department takes the database established by the design department and enriches it with production data and information to produce a plan for the production of the product. Planning involves several subsystems dealing with materials, facility, process, tools, manpower, capacity, scheduling, outsourcing, assembly, inspection, logistics etc. In a CIM system, this planning process should be constrained by the production costs and by the production equipment and process capability, in order to generate an optimized plan.

子系统
人力 / 能力 / 调度 / 外包 / 装配
检测 / 物流

4.4 Purchase 采购

The purchase departments is responsible for placing the orders and follow up, ensure quality in the production process of the vendor, receive the items, arrange for inspection and supply the items to the stores or arrange timely delivery depending on the production schedule for eventual supply to manufacture and assembly.

发出订单
跟进 / 供货商
及时交货 / 生产计划

4.5 Manufacturing Engineering 制造工程

Manufacturing Engineering is the activity of carrying out the production of the product, involving further enrichment of the database with performance data and information about the production equipment and processes. In CIM, this requires activities like CNC programming, simulation and computer aided scheduling of the production activity. This should include online dynamic scheduling and control based on the real time performance of the equipment and processes to assure continuous production activity. Often, the need to meet fluctuating market demand requires the manufacturing system flexible and agile.

调度
实时
确保
波动
敏捷的

4.6 Factory Automation Hardware 工厂自动化硬件

Factory automation equipment further enriches the database with equipment and process data. In CIM system this consists of computer controlled process machinery such as CNC machine tools, flexible manufacturing systems (FMS), computer controlled robots, material handling systems, computer controlled assembly systems, flexibly

加工机械

automated inspection systems and so on.

4.7 Warehousing 仓储

Warehousing is the function involving storage and retrieval of raw materials, components, finished goods as well as shipment of items. In today's complex outsourcing scenario and the need for just-in-time supply of components and subsystems, logistics and supply chain management assume great importance.

4.8 Finance 财务

Finance deals with the resources pertaining to money. Planning of investment, working capital, and cash flow control, realization of receipts, accounting and allocation of funds are the major tasks of the finance departments.

4.9 Information Management 信息管理

Information Management is perhaps one of the crucial tasks in CIM. This involves master production scheduling, database management, communication, manufacturing systems integration and management information systems. It can be seen from Fig. 9.2 that CIM technology ties together all the manufacturing and related

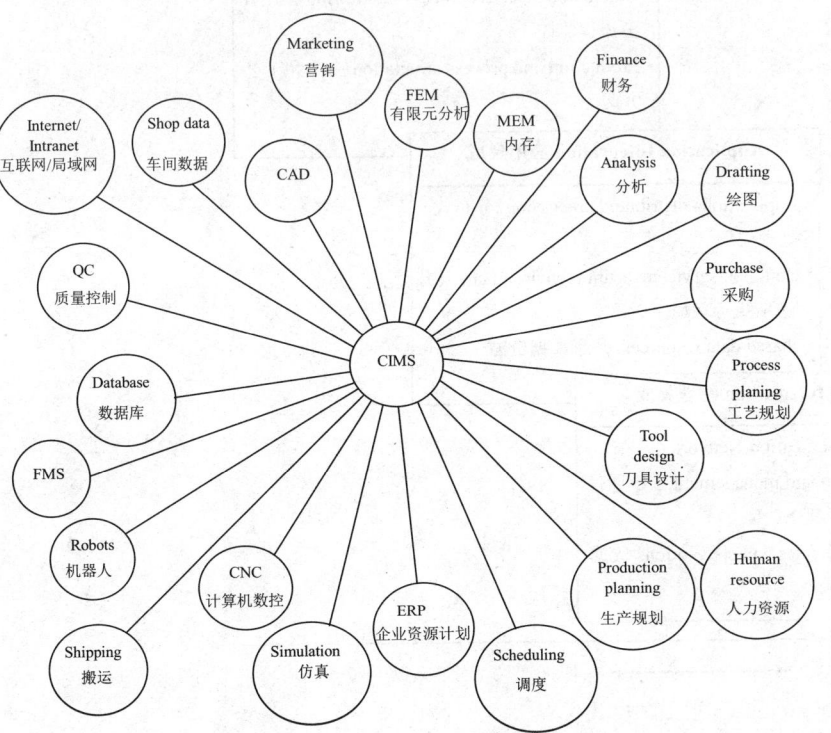

Fig. 9.2 Various activities in CIMS

functions in a company. Implementation of CIM technology thus involves basically integration of all the activities of the enterprise.

5. Levels of Integration in CIMS   CIMS 集成的级别

CIM is an integration process leading to the integration of the manufacturing enterprise. Fig. 9.3 indicates different levels of this integration that can be seen within an industry. <u>Dictated</u> by the needs of the individual enterprise this process usually starts with the need to <u>interchange</u> information between the some of the so called islands of automation. Flexible manufacturing cells, automatic storage and retrieval systems, CAD/CAM based design etc are the examples of islands of automation. This involves data exchange among computers, NC machines, robots, <u>gantry</u> systems etc. Therefore the integration process has started <u>bottom up</u>. The <u>interconnection</u> of physical systems is the first requirement to be recognized and fulfilled.

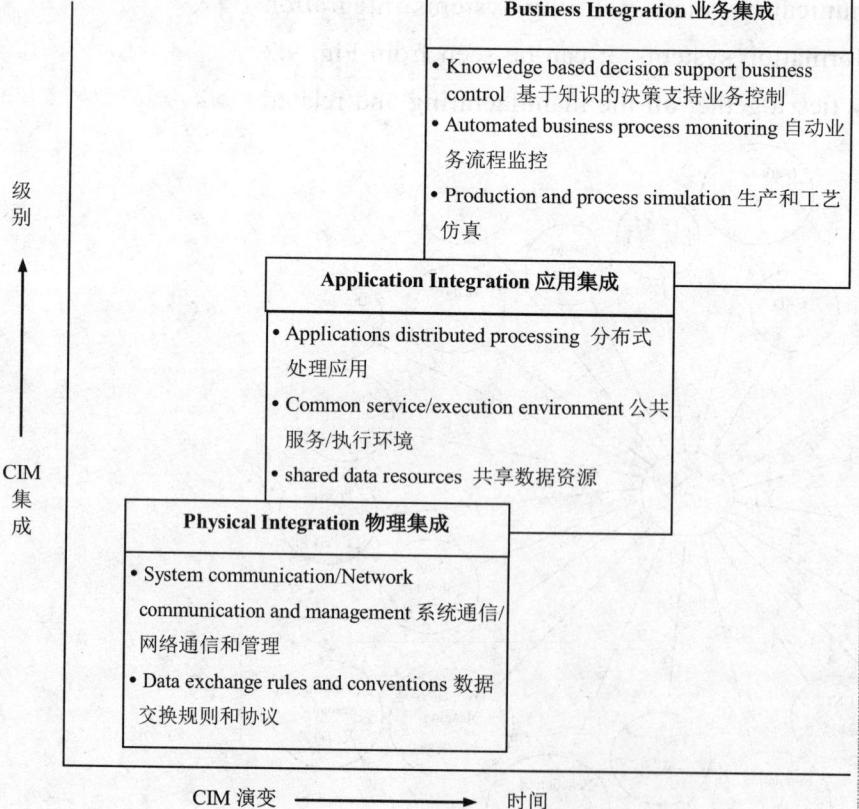

Fig. 9.3 Levels of integration of CIMS

The next level of integration, application integration in Fig. 9.3 is concerned with the integration of applications, the term applications being used in the data processing sense. The applications are those which are discussed in section 4 under the heading CIM hardware and software. Application integration involves supply and retrieval of information between users and system itself. Thus the application integration level imposes constraints on the physical integration level. There has to be control of the applications themselves also.

取出
施加

The highest level of integration, business integration in Fig. 9.3 is concerned with the management and operational processes of an enterprise. The management process provides supervisory control of the operational process which in turn co-ordinates the day-to-day execution of the activities at the application level. The business integration level therefore places constraints on the application level. This level offers considerable challenge to the integration activity.

监管
协调

专业词汇

computer integrated manufacturing system(CIMS) 计算机集成制造系统
performance 性能
scheduled delivery date 计划交货期
total quality management 全面质量管理
business process reengineering 业务流程重组
concurrent engineering 并行工程
mass customization 大批量定制
manufacturing industry 制造业
on time delivery 准时交货
outsourcing 外包
robotized work cell 自动化工作单元
heterogeneous 异构的
aerospace industry 航空工业
innovation 创新
mainframe computer 大型机
microprocessor 微处理器
hierarchical 层次

geometric modeling 几何建模
accounting 会计
marketing 市场营销
workstation 工作站
terminal 终端
bar code reader 条形码阅读器
RFID tag 无线射频识别标签
peripheral device 外围设备
shop floor data collection 车间数据采集
order entry 订单录入
business process management 业务流程管理
warehousing 仓储
logistics and supply chain management 物流与供应链管理
vendor 供货商
production schedule 生产计划

inventory control 库存控制
co-ordinate measuring machine 坐标测量机
cash flow 现金流
supervisory 监管

思考题：

1. 在制造业全球化背景下，CIMS 需要实现的目标是什么？
2. CIMS 如何消除制造业中的自动化孤岛？
3. 简述 CIMS 的发展演变过程。
4. CIMS 包含哪些硬件和软件？
5. 描述在 CIMS 中有哪些不同的元素？各有何作用？
6. 简述物理集成、应用集成和业务集成的不同之处，并举例说明。

Chapter 10　Industrial Robot Technology
工业机器人技术

1. Industrial Robots　工业机器人

There are a variety of definitions of the term robot. Depending on the definition used, the number of robot installations worldwide varies widely. Although several different production machines may appear to have the capacity to work like a robot, on closer inspection the robot is distinctly different. The International Standards Organization defines an industrial robot as follows: A robot is an automatically controlled, reprogrammable, multipurpose, manipulating machine with several reprogrammable axes, which may be either fixed in place or mobile for use in industrial automation applications. The key words are reprogrammable and multipurpose because most single-purpose machines do not meet these two requirements. Reprogrammable implies two characteristics: (1) the robot's motion is controlled by a written program and (2) the program can be modified to change the motion of the robot significantly. Multipurpose emphasizes the fact that a robot can perform many different functions, depending on the program and tooling currently in use. For example, a robot could be tooled and programmed in one company to do welding, and in a second company the same type of robot could be used to stack boxes.

Introduced in the early 1960s, the first industrial robots were used in hazardous operations, such as the handling of toxic and radioactive materials and the loading and unloading of hot workpieces from furnaces and in foundries. Some simple rule-of-thumb applications for robots are the three D's (dull, dirty, and dangerous) and three H's (hot, heavy, and hazardous). From their early uses for worker protection and safety in manufacturing plants, industrial robots have further been developed and have now become important components in

---

可重复编程的 / 多用途的 / 可操纵的

焊接
堆叠
装箱

危险的 / 有毒的 / 有辐射的

熔炉 / 铸造厂 / 经验法则
枯燥的

manufacturing processes and systems. They have helped to improve productivity and product quality and to reduce labor costs. Computer-controlled robots were commercialized in the early 1970s. The first robot controlled by a microcomputer appeared in 1974.

2. Robot Components 机器人的组成

To appreciate the functions of robot components and their capabilities, we might simultaneously observe the flexibility and capability of diverse movements of our arm, wrist, hand, and fingers in reaching for and grabbing an object from a shelf, or in using a hand tool, or in operating a machine. Described next are the basic components of an industrial robot.

2.1 Manipulator 操作机构

The manipulator (also called arm and wrist) is a mechanical section that provides motions similar to those of a human arm and hand. The end of the wrist can reach a point in space having a specific set of coordinates, in a specific orientation. Most robots have six rotational joints. There are also four degrees of freedom (DOF) and five DOF robots, but these kinds, by definition, are not fully dextrous, because being so requires six DOF. Seven DOF (or "redundant") robots for special applications are also available. Manipulation is carried out using mechanical devices, such as linkages, gears, and various joints.

2.2 End Effector 终端执行机构

The end of the wrist in a robot is equipped with an end effector. Depending on the type of operation, conventional end effectors may be equipped with any of the following: (1) grippers, electromagnets, and vacuum cups, for material handling; (2) spray guns, for painting; (3) attachments, for spot and arc welding and for arc cutting; (4) power tools, such as drills; (5)measuring instruments, such as dial indicators. End effectors are generally custom-made to meet special handling requirements. Mechanical grippers are the most commonly used and equipped with two or more fingers. The selection of an appropriate end effector for a specific application depends on such factors as the payload, environment, reliability and cost. Compliant end effectors are used to handle fragile materials or to facilitate assembly. These end effectors can use elastic mechanisms to limit the force which can be applied to the workpiece, or they can be designed with a desired stiffness.

有效载荷 / 柔顺的
脆性 / 便于装配
弹性的
刚度

2.3 Power Supply 动力源

Each motion of the manipulator (in linear and rotational axes) is controlled by independent actuators that use an electrical, a pneumatic, or a hydraulic power supply. Each source of energy and each type of motor has its own characteristics, advantages, and limitations.

执行机构 / 气动的
液压的

2.4 Control System 控制系统

The control system is the communications and information-processing system that gives commands for the movements of the robot. It is the brain of the robot, it stores data to initiate and terminate movements of the manipulator. It is also the nerves of the robot, it interfaces with computers and other equipment such as manufacturing cells or assembly systems. The manipulators and end effectors are the robot's arms and hands. Feedback devices, such as transducers, are an important part of the control system. Robots with a fixed set of motions have open-loop control. In this system commands are given and the robot arm goes through its motions; unlike feedback in closed-loop systems, accuracy of the movements is not monitored. Consequently, this system does not have a self-correcting capability.

终止
机械手 / 神经
传感器
开环

3. Classification of Robots 机器人的分类

Robots may be classified as follows:

(1) Cartesian or rectilinear 笛卡尔形或直线形

A robot with a Cartesian geometry can move its gripper to any position within the cube or rectangle defined as its working volume. The rectangular work envelope of this type of robot is often used to move parts from conveyor systems into production machines (see Fig. 10.1 (a)).

立方体
范围
传送带

(2) Cylindrical 圆柱形

Cylindrical coordinate robot, like the one illustrated in Fig. 10.1(b), can move the gripper within a volume that is described by a cylinder. The cylindrical coordinate robot system is positioned in the work area by two linear movements and one angular rotation. The axes on cylindrical coordinate robots are driven <u>pneumatically</u>, hydraulically or electrically.

(3) Spherical or polar 球形或两极形

The spherical geometry robot, sometimes called polar, is drawn in Fig. 10.1 (c). Spherical arm geometry robots position the wrist through two rotations and one linear <u>actuation</u>.

(4) Articulated or jointed 铰接形或关节形

Articulated industrial robots have two main variants, <u>vertically</u> articulated and <u>horizontally</u> articulated. The vertically articulated robot (Fig. 10.1 (d)) has three major <u>angular</u> movements consisting of a base rotation, shoulder, and <u>forearm</u> joint. The <u>orientation</u> of the tool plate is provided by the three rotations in the <u>wrist</u>. Electric drives with feedback control systems are used on most machines.

An example of a <u>jointed-spherical</u> configuration is illustrated in Fig. 10.2.

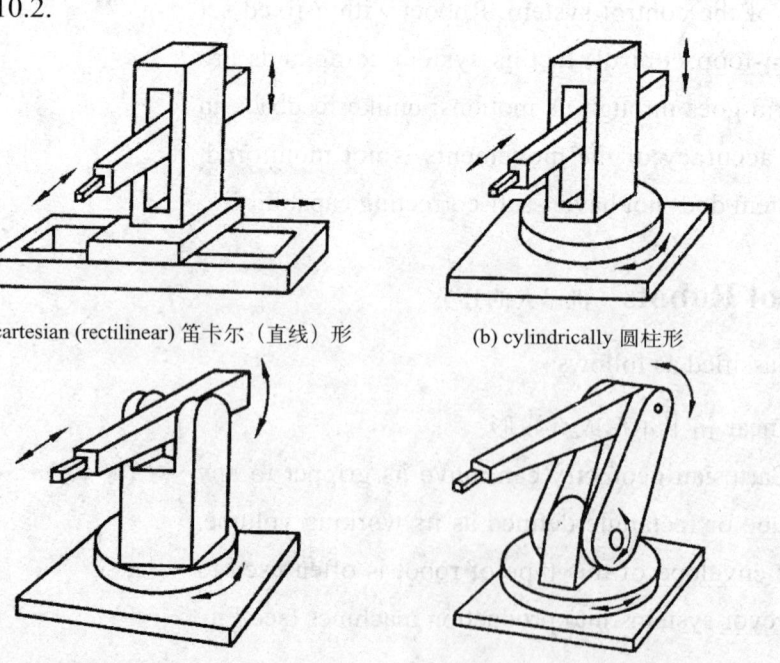

(a) cartesian (rectilinear) 笛卡尔（直线）形　　(b) cylindrically 圆柱形

(c) spherical (polar) 球（极）形　　(d) articulated (jointed) 铰接（关节）形

Fig. 10.1 Four types of industrial robots

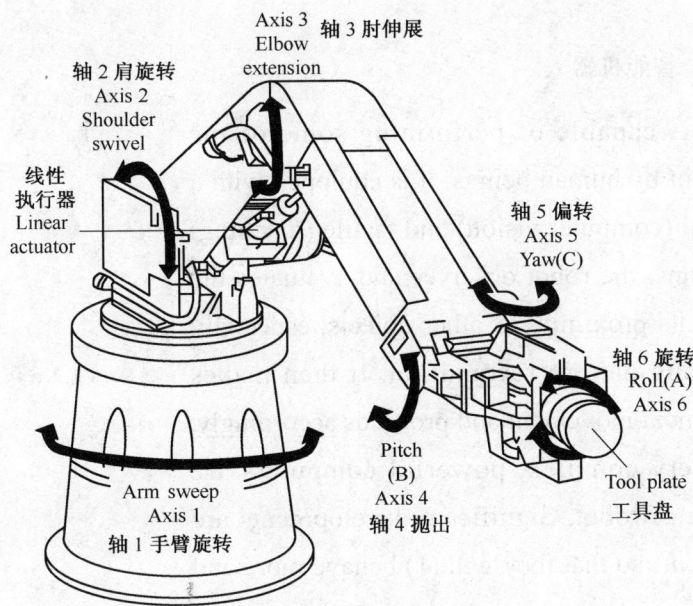

Fig. 10.2 Joint-spherical robot

Robots may be <u>attached</u> permanently to the floor of a manufacturing plant, or they may move along <u>overhead rails</u>, or they may be equipped with wheels to move along the factory floor. A broader classification of robots currently in use is described below.

Fixed-Sequence Robots. The fixed-sequence robot (also called a pick-and-place robot) is programmed for a specific sequence of operations. Robot that once programmed for a given sequence of operations is not easily changed. Its movements are from point to point, and the cycle is repeated continuously. These robots are simple and relatively inexpensive.

Variable-Sequence Robots. The variable-sequence robot can be programmed for a specific sequence of operations and can easily be changed or reprogrammed to perform another sequence of operation.

Playback Robots. Playback robot can memorizes and records the path and sequence of motions taught by a human being who physically leads the device through the intended work pattern and can repeat them continually without any further action or guidance by the operator.

4. Intelligent Robots 智能机器人

The intelligent robot is capable of performing some of the functions and tasks carried out by human beings. It is equipped with a variety of sensors with visual (computer vision) and tactile (touching) capabilities. Much like humans, the robot observes and evaluates the immediate environment and its proximity to other objects, especially machinery, by perception and pattern recognition. It then makes appropriate decisions for the next movement and proceeds accordingly. Because its operation is very complex, powerful computers are required to control this type of robot. Significant developments are taking place in intelligent robots so that they will (1) behave more and more like humans, performing tasks such as moving among a variety of machines and equipment on the shop floor and avoiding collisions; (2) recognize, select, and properly grip the correct raw material or workpiece; (3) transport the part to a machine for further processing or inspection; (4) assemble the components into subassemblies or a final product.

5. Applications and Selection of Robots
机器人的应用和选择

Major applications of industrial robots include the following: (1) Material handing consists of the loading, unloading, and transferring of workpieces in manufacturing facilities. These operations can be performed reliably and repeatedly with robots. Here are some examples: (a) casting and molding operations, in which molten metal, raw materials lubricants, and parts in various stages of manufacture are handled without operator interference; (b) heat treating, in which parts are loaded and unloaded from furnaces and quench baths; (c) forming operations, in which parts are loaded and unloaded from presses and various other types of metalworking machinery. (2) Spot welding produce welds of good quality in the manufacture of automobile and truck bodies. Robots also perform other similar operations, such as arc welding, arc cutting, and riveting. (3) Operations such as deburring, grinding, and polishing can be done by using appropriate tools attached to the end effectors. (4) Spray painting (particularly of complex shapes) and cleaning operations are frequent applications because the motions for one piece repeat so accurately for the next. (5) Automated assembly is again very repetitive. (6) Inspection and gaging in various stages of manufacture make possible speeds much higher than those humans can achieve.

Factors that influence the selection of robots in manufacturing are as follows: (1) Load-carrying capacity; (2) Speed of movement; (3) Reliability; (4) Repeatability; (5) Arm configuration; (6) Degrees of freedom; (7) The control system; (8) Program memory; (9) Work envelope.

In addition to the technical factors, cost and benefit considerations are also significant aspects of robot selection and their use. The increasing availability and reliability, and the reduced costs, of sophisticated, intelligent robots are having a major economic impact on manufacturing operations, and such robots are gradually displacing human labor.

Depending on the size of the robot's work envelope, its speed, and its proximity to humans, safety considerations in a robot environment may be important, particularly for programmers and maintenance personnel who are in direct physical interaction with robots. In addition, the movement of the robot with respect to other machinery requires a high level of reliability in order to avoid collisions and serious damage to equipment. Its material-handling activities require proper securing of raw material and parts in the robot gripper at various stages in the production line.

专业词汇

rule-of-thumb 经验法则
manipulator 操作机构、机械手
coordinate 坐标
joint 关节
power supply 动力源
actuator 执行机构
transducer 传感器
open-loop control 开环控制

degrees of freedom (DOF) 自由度
dextrous 灵巧的
linkage 连接
gear 齿轮
end effector 终端执行机构
gripper 卡爪
electromagnet 电磁铁
vacuum cup 真空吸盘
attachment 附件
spot welding 点焊
arc welding 弧焊
dial indicators 千分尺
payload 有效载荷
fragile material 脆性材料
elastic 弹性的
stiffness 刚度

Cartesian 笛卡尔的
rectilinear 直线的
cylindrical 圆柱形的
spherical 球形的
articulated 铰接的
forearm 前臂
sensor 传感器
tactile 触觉
perception 感知
pattern recognition 模式识别
casting and molding 铸造成型
lubricant 润滑剂
arc cutting 电弧切割
deburring 倒角
spray painting 喷漆

思考题：

1. 国际标准组织 ISO 对工业机器人是如何定义的？如何理解该定义？
2. 机器人应用的经验法则是什么？
3. 工业机器人由哪几部分组成？简述各部分的组成和作用。
4. 工业机器人分为哪四种类型？各应用在什么场合？
5. 工业机器人主要应用在哪些方面？请举例说明。

Chapter 11　Automatic Detection and Monitoring Technology 自动检测与监控技术

1. Introduction to Automatic Detection of Weld Defects 焊接缺陷自动检测

X-ray imaging is a widely used technique for inspection of industrial pieces and for the medical diagnosis of human diseases. Traditional radiographic testing with film is an expensive and time-consuming technique. Therefore, digital radioscopy that permits real-time inspection has been developed and applied. Now, experienced workers are required to evaluate the moving weld seam based on the video displayed on monitor. The manual interpretation process can be subjective, inconsistent, and easily cause fatigue. Therefore, it is imperative to develop an automatic computer-aided system to increase the objectivity, consistency and efficiency of defect inspection. Now, automatic detection of defects in real-time digital RT system consists of two aspects: (1) identifying the defects in the weld, (2) classifying different types of welding defects.

When weld seam is moving, weld defects are very thin and do not have a high contrast under X-rays. Defects inspection at this condition is a very challenging problem. To the best of our knowledge, no commercially real-time automatic RT system exists today. On-line inspection requires a computationally fast and effective method, therefore the main task is now focused on the identifying and locating flaws in the moving weld. Classifying is not possible due to computational cost and time-consumption. In the process of locating and detecting defects, we always fall into the dilemma between locating all the true defects and avoiding any false alarms.

2. Component Structure of the System 系统组成架构

The system consists of conversion part, processing part and serial communication part as shown in Fig. 11.1 The conversion part consists of X-ray source, weld seam, transmission vehicle, intensifier and CCD camera. The function of this part is to make the conversion from X-ray to visible light. Firstly, X-ray is transferred into visual light through light intensifier. Then the CCD camera transfers the light signal into electric signal and sends it to the processing part. The processing part consists of monitor, image grabber, computer, and computer screen. In this part, the electric signal is sampled and transformed into digital signal by image grabber, and at the same time it is also displayed on the monitor. The digital image is sent into the computer and will be detected using the defect detection algorithm based on fuzzy recognition theory. The result will be displayed on computer screen in real-time and stored in computer for future check or test. The serial communication part consists of Single Chip Microcomputer, rotary coder, serial communication, optical isolator module and transmission device, etc. The function of this part is to obtain and transmit the information of position. The system transforms the displaced signal into the pulse signal utilizing the rotary coder and attains displacement by computing the number of the pulse. Then the displacement signal

转换

增强器

图像采集卡
采样

算法/模糊识别

单片机/旋转编码器
串行通信/光学隔离模块/传输设备

脉冲/得到

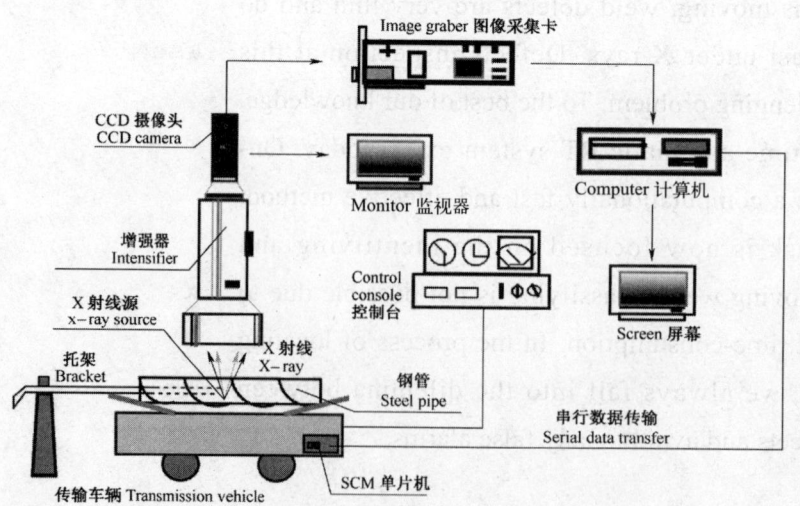

Fig. 11.1 The component structure of the system

系统的组成结构

is transmitted to the computer for the defects location through serial communication.

3. Principle of Automatic Detection 自动检测原理

The defects detection includes two main procedures: image preprocessing and realization of the algorithm. The detailed explanations are as follows.

Extraction of the Weld Seam 焊缝信号的提取

Usually, an automatic welding process yields a relatively uniform weld. Since only the items within a weld are of interest for the purpose of image processing, this system extracted the weld area free of background. This system has the prior information about brightness distribution in the points of object and background. There are three main areas in the weld image, the base metal area, the weld area, and lead plate area. The weld seam is oriented along the horizontal direction.

After welds are successfully extracted, it is then to identify the defect areas. X-ray imaging is inherently noisy because of the quantum nature of radiation, there may be only a few photons per pixel per exposure time. Large defects can be easily detected by many methods. But small defects encounter the difficulty of differentiation between true defects pixels and noisy impulses. On this condition, the performance of typical methods is not good as compared to a human operator. In order to achieve fast and precise detection, a region-based approach that imitates visual inspection is used. In the weld image, defects appear brighter as typical weld defects are lack of matter. A volumetric defect appears as a bright blob, while a planar defect appears as a bright line in the image. For visual inspection, contrast and variance are important because the human visual system is very sensitive to the two parameters. Under the circumstance of a fixed contrast, the smaller the variance of an area is, the more reasonable it is a defect area. To a fixed variance, the higher the contrast of an area is, the more possible is the defect presence. The contrast is usually given by the gray-level difference between the object and its neighborhoods. This is the principle of fuzzy algorithm, from which fuzzy rules applied in defect detection algorithm comes. The concrete defects detection algorithm is as follow.

In detection of blowhole and slag inclusion, the sizes of contrast and detection area are selected as 10×3 and 6×4. The contrast areas are divided into two groups, the horizontal distances between the two groups and the detect area are $5 - 8$ and $15 - 18$ pixels; the vertical contrast area is also divided into two groups, the distance between the two groups and the detect area respectively are $3 - 6$ and $8 - 11$ pixels, the sketch of detect area and contrast area is shown as Fig. 11.2 Although the method of detecting incomplete penetration is the same as blowhole or slag inclusion, an incomplete penetration is not like a blowhole or slag inclusion that shows a bright point, but shows a bright line. So in detection of lack of penetration, the detect area is selected as 2×20 pixels. After obtaining the two groups' average gray level, add them up and make an average to get the average gray level of the contrast area. Then we can get the average gray level difference A by subtracting the average gray level of the contrast area from that of the detected area. Thirdly a square of the difference between average gray level of detect area and the gray level value of every point in the detected area is made. At last, by adding all of obtained squares up and make an average of them we will get the variance V of the detected area.

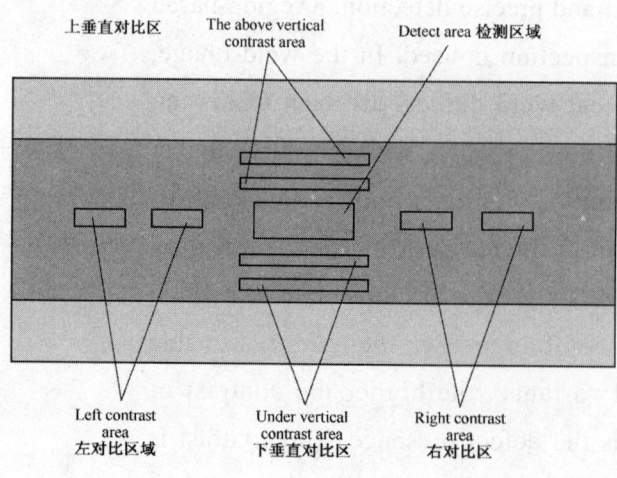

Fig. 11.2 The detected area

4. Application in the Factory 工厂应用

In the factory, this system had run for more than half a year, which have detected several kinds of defects, such as porosities, slags, incomplete penetration. A total of 216 was selected, among which 136 are porosities, the smallest of which is 400mm, 75 are slags, five are incomplete penetration. The performance of detection is equal to the evaluation of a human operator. As an illustration of the whole method, there are five examples of incomplete penetration, which is a typical type of weld defect quite hard to detect. Fig. 11.3(a) and (c) shows a part of such a raw image; Fig. 11.3(b) and (d) shows detected objects denoted by black line.

孔隙／矿渣

表示

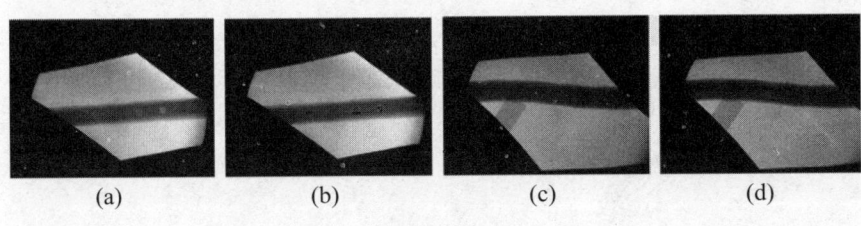

(a)　　　　(b)　　　　(c)　　　　(d)

Fig. 11.3 The actual detection

实际检测

X-ray weld seam automatic detection system applies defect detection algorithm based on fuzzy rules to identify defects in welded seam. It can give a very high confidence about the defect, but rough information on type. The proposed method based on fuzzy rules avoids many drawbacks of traditional approaches.

粗糙

专业词汇

X-ray imaging　X 射线成像
radiographic testing　射线照相测试
radioscopy　射线透视
weld seam　焊缝
fatigue　疲劳
defects inspection　缺陷检测
flaw　瑕疵
image grabber　图像采集卡
algorithm　算法

rotary coder　旋转编码器
serial communication　串行通信
optical isolator module　光学隔离模块
extract　提取
differentiation　区别
contrast　对比度
gray-level　灰度级
blowhole　气孔
slag inclusion　夹渣

fuzzy recognition 模糊识别
single chip microcomputer 单片机
porosity 孔隙
rough 粗糙的

思考题：

1. 简述工业生产中使用自动检测和监控系统的必要性。
2. 焊接缺陷自动检测系统主要由哪几部分组成？说明该系统的工作原理。
3. 如何辨别焊缝图像中存在缺陷的区域？

Part III

Modern Production and Management Technology

现代生产管理技术

Chapter 12　Product Data Management
产品数据管理

1. Introduction　简介

　　Product Data Management (PDM) systems are increasingly being utilized in industrial applications for long-term archival of product information, to enhance collaboration and communication throughout the design process, support distributed design teams through advanced document sharing, track changes in product information, and control design documents ranging from requirements information to CAD.

　　The adoption of PDM systems has caused a change in how design processes are managed and how individual designers collaborate. Additionally, companies are pushing the limits of currently available PDM software resulting in continual development and new application domains. For example, commercial software vendors have integrated PDM systems with other design support tools, included automated workflow management, and suites of CAD/CAM/CAE tools, refined and developed new functionality.

| 产品数据管理 |
| 档案 |
| 协作 |
| 分布式的 |
| 文档共享 / 跟踪 |
| 采用 |
| 个人 / 协作 |
| 另外 |
| 领域 / 提供商 / 集成 |
| 工作流管理 / 套件 / 完善 |

2. The Function of PDM　PDM 的功能

　　PDM as a suitable data management solution, the following key requirements have been identified:

　　(1) Document management. The system should be able to store any type of electronic file. With each file, meta data should be associated to allow for an easy retrieval. The system should enable the long-term preservation of all data. In addition, the system should be able to associate different documents with one another and arrange them in a hierarchical structure.

　　(2) CAD model support. Apart from providing preview functionality for CAD models, the system should also be able to

| 解决方案 |
| 文档管理 |
| 元数据 |
| 关联 / 检索 / 使能 |
| 保存 |
| 层次结构 |
| CAD 模型支持 / 除了 / 预览功能 |

capture aggregation hierarchies of CAD files. "Is-part-of" associations are especially important to reflect the relationships between CAD files.

(3) Access control. Read/write access to files should be granted to authorize persons only. Therefore, sophisticated rights management must be available. All access to files should be tracked.

(4) Concurrency control. The system should either prevent concurrent modifications of documents or provide a means of merging different versions. This particularly applies to CAD files which are subject to intensive collaborative work.

(5) Version control. The system should be able to track the version history of a document and provide a way of identifying who has changed what at which time. It is especially important to associate corresponding versions of different documents that are related to each other. Also a rollback functionality should be provided, both for single document and for a network of interrelated documents.

(6) Workflow support. A status should be assignable to each document (such as in work, approved, released). For each state, it should be possible to define who is authorized to access, modify or delete the document. Status changes initiated by a user should optionally invoke one or more actions to be performed by the system, such as notifying the succeeding person in charge by e-mail.

(7) User interface. The user interface should provide easy access to the system, comprehensive search features, and preview functionality for the most typical file formats. A web interface should allow access to the system from any computer or mobile device.

(8) Federated system. Each of the organizations or companies involved should have an individual data management system forming part of a decentralized architecture. When a document is released and handed over from one party to another, it has to be duplicated and transmitted to the target system. This ensures that the hand-over is clearly documented.

These demands form the basis for assessing and evaluating PDM systems as a data management solution for not only industry but also service.

3. Integrating Product Data Through SSPD
通过单一来源集成产品数据

The increasing product diversity and sophistication have demanded an integrated system which can integrate subsystems of an enterprise. Our purpose is to efficiently use all resources available in a manufacturing enterprise by developing a fully integrated system. The proposed system uses the electronic data processing methods together with new database techniques. A framework based on single source of product data (SSPD) system is established to completely integrate the different subsystem of production line. The SSPD framework describe the product data generation, transmission and processing of a production line. The SSPD system validation is carried out by implementing the system in Ford Motor Company.

During the process of product evolution, a huge amount of data information is generated and stored. At the initial stage of engineering design, process exposes a number of problems like configuration and change management, and overall management of digital data. Sometimes two or more records of the same set of product attributes, components found in numerous locations which cause redundancy in the data. This redundancy occupies a lot of storage space and difficult to access accurate data. A single source product data reduces the redundancy to the minimum level in the huge product data record of an enterprise. Data inconsistency is another problem created by redundancy. During updating or change of data, it may change in one location and may not update the same data at all locations but this problem also minimizing by using the SSPD.

Configuration management is also very important during the process of product evolution. In SSPD products can be adjusted in the functional structure and composition without redesigning as per customer requirements. With a well-organized configuration management method, an enterprises can have the dexterity they require to promptly define and produce new products as per customer expectations. The integrity constraints are also set under certain rules to improve the effectively of the system.

4. PDM at Ford Motor Company   PDM 在福特汽车公司的应用

Over ten years ago, Ford Motor Company implemented a PDM system worldwide. It was part of a new CAD initiative which Ford called C3P, an acronym for CAD/CAM/CAE/PIM. PIM (Product Information Management) is a Ford-specific term for PDM. Although this project was called C3P, Ford's focus in this endeavor was on the PDM system. This project began in 1996, and by mid-1998, 16 vehicle programs had already begun using the new system. Ford's plans were to use the PDM system worldwide, so that all of its operations and suppliers accessed CAD files that were stored in Dearborn, Michigan. Ford's C3P program was a $200 million deal with SDRC (the parent company of IDEAS and Metaphase), which included both software and services. Before this deal, Ford had used other CAD and PDM systems, including a PDM system developed in-house. Ford's expectations for the new PDM system were very high and they saw results very quickly. Ford experienced the obvious improvement, which was a faster time-to-market of its products. Engineering efficiency rose around 30% – 40% due to new solid modeling capabilities. This increase in efficiency has the potential to save one program as much as $100 million. Prototype costs decreased by 40% – 50%, saving hundreds of millions of dollars. Late changes were reduced by 50%, and programs were able to be completed in less than two years. Ford was able to extend the benefits of C3P beyond the design of the vehicle itself. They used computer programs to analyze the solid models in order to determine a vehicle's manufacturability within an existing plant. In one case, Ford was able to prevent a $60 million tooling modification that would have been required had the design not been analyzed ahead of time. Ford's C3P program was a success that continues today. Thus, by implementing a PDM system, Ford was able to (1) reduce time to market of new vehicles, (2) increase engineering efficiency, (3) reduce prototype costs, (4) reduce late changes to parts.

专业词汇

product data management(PDM) 产品数据管理
collaboration 协作
distributed 分布式的
document sharing 文档共享
vendor 提供商
integrated 集成的
workflow 工作流
solution 解决方案
meta data 元数据
retrieval 检索
enable 使能
preservation 保存
hierarchical structure 层次结构
preview 预览
aggregation 聚合
access control 访问控制
authorize 授权
rights management 权限管理
concurrency control 并发控制
merge 合并
collaborative work 协同工作
version control 版本控制
rollback 回滚
approve 批准
release 释放
access 访问
invoke 调用
architecture 架构
duplicate 复制
database techniques 数据库技术
framework 框架
production line 生产线
implement 实现
configuration 配置
storage space 存储空间
inconsistency 不一致
manufacturability 可制造性
tooling 工装

思考题：

1. 简述 PDM 系统的主要功能。
2. 如何通过单一来源实现产品数据集成？
3. 以福特汽车公司为例说明实施 PDM 为企业带来的好处。

Chapter 13 Manufacturing Resource Planning
制造资源计划

1. Material Requirements Planning 物料需求计划

MRP is a dependent demand technique that uses bill of material, inventory, expected receipts, and a master production schedule to determine material requirements. Our emphasis here is on material requirements planning(MRP), which is the key piece of logic that ties the production functions together from a material planning. MRP has been installed almost universally in manufacturing firms, even those considered small. The reason is that MRP is a logical, easily understandable approach to the problem of determining the number of parts, components, and material needed to produce each end item. MRP also provides the schedule specifying when each of these items should be ordered or produced. MRP has evolved as the basis for Enterprise Resource Planning(ERP).

依赖需求/物料清单
库存/预期投入/主生产计划

联系
普遍地/公司

零件/部件

演变
企业资源计划

2. Dependent Inventory Model Requirements
依赖库存模型需求

MRP is based on dependent demand. By dependent demand, we mean that the demand for one item is related to the demand for another item. Consider the Ford Explorer, Ford's demand for auto tires and radiators depends on the production of Explorers. Four tires and one radiator go into each finished Explorer. Demand for items is dependent when the relationship between the items can be determined. Therefore, once management receives an order or makes a forecast of the demand for the final product, quantities required for all components can be computed, because all components are dependent items. More generally, for any item for which a schedule can be established, dependent techniques should be used.

Effective use of dependent inventory models requires that the

产品
福特探险者汽车/汽车/轮胎
散热器

零部件

operations manager know the following: (1) Master production schedule (what is to be made and when), (2) Specifications or bill of material (materials and parts required to make the product), (3) Inventory availability (what is in stock), (4) Purchase orders (what is on order), (5) Lead times (how long it takes to get various components). We now discuss each of these requirements in the context of material requirements planning(MRP).

主生产计划
规范 / 物料清单
库存量 / 库存 / 采购订单
提前期

2.1 Master Production Schedule 主生产计划

A master production schedule (MPS) specifies what is to be made (i.e., the number of finished products or items) and when. The schedule must be in accordance with a production plan. The production plan sets the overall level of output in broad terms (for example, product families, standard hours, or dollar volume). The plan also includes a variety of inputs, including financial plans, customer demand, engineering capabilities, labor availability, inventory fluctuations, supplier performance, and other considerations.

一致的
整体水平
标准工时 / 成交金额
财务计划
劳动力供应 / 库存波动
供应商绩效

The upper portion of Fig. 13.1 shows an aggregate plan for the total number of mattresses planned per month, without regard for mattress type. The lower portion shows a master production schedule specifying the exact type of mattress and the quantity planned for production by week. The next level down (not shown) would be the MRP program that develops detailed schedules showing when cotton batting, springs, and hardwood are needed to make the mattresses.

上部分 / 总计划
床垫
指定 / 准确的
棉絮
弹簧 / 硬木

Aggregate Production Plan for Mattresses 床垫总生产计划

Month 月	1	2
Mattress Production 床垫产量	900	950

型号 / 周	1	2	3	4	5	6	7	8
Model 327	200			400		200	100	
Model 538		100	100		150		100	
Model 749			100			200		200

Master Production Schedule for Mattress Models 床垫型号主生产计划

Fig. 13.1 The Aggregate Plan and the Master Production Schedule for Mattresses 床垫总计划和主生产计划

To again summarize the planning sequence, the aggregate operations plan specifies product groups. It does not specify exact items. The next level down in the planning process is the master production schedule. The master production schedule is the time-phased plan specifying how many and when the firm plans to build each end item. For example, the aggregate plan for a furniture company may specify the total volume of mattresses it plans to produce over the next month or next quarter. The MPS goes the next step down and identifies the exact size mattresses and their qualities and styles. All of the mattresses sold by the company would be specified by the MPS. The MPS also states period by period (usually weekly) how many and when each of these mattress types is needed.

Still further down the disaggregation process is the MRP program, which calculates and schedules all raw materials, parts, and supplies needed to make the mattress specified by the MPS. Generally, the master schedule deals with end items and is a major input to the MRP process. If the end item is quite large or quite expensive, however, the master production schedule may schedule major subassemblies or components instead. The master production schedule can be expressed in any of the following terms: (1) A customer order in a job shop (make-to-order) company. (2) Modules in a repetitive (assemble-to-order or forecast) company. (3) An end item in a continuous (stock-to-forecast) company. This relationship of the master production schedule to the processes is shown in Fig. 13.2.

2.2 Bill of Material 物料清单

The bill of materials(BOM) file contains the complete product description, listing not only the materials, parts, and components but also the sequence in which the product is created. This BOM file is one of the three main inputs to the MRP program. (The other two are the master schedule and the inventory records file).

One way a bill of material defines a product is by providing a product structure. Example 1 shows how to develop the product structure and "explode" it to reveal the requirements for each component. A bill of material for item A in Example 1 consists of

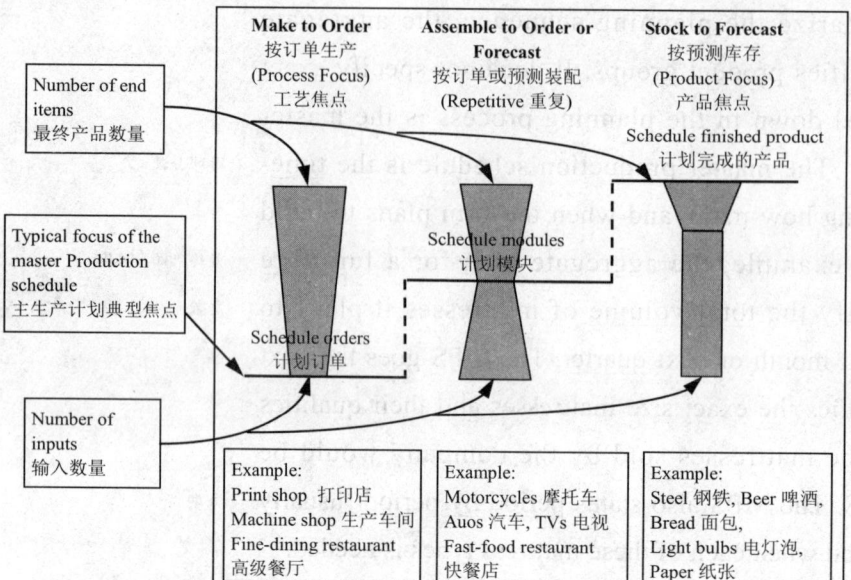

Fig. 13.2 Typical Focus of the Master Production Schedule in Three Process Strategies

三个过程策略中主生产计划的典型焦点

items B and C. Items above any level are called parents. Items below any level are called components or children.

Example 1: Speaker Kits, Inc., packages high-fidelity components for mail order. Components for the top-of-the-line speaker kit, "Awesome" (A), include 2 standard 12-inch speaker kits (Bs) and 3 speaker kits with amp boosters (Cs), and so on. As we can see, the demand for B, C, D, E, F, and G is completely dependent on the master production schedule for A-the Awesome speaker kits. Given this information, we can construct the following product structure in Fig. 13.3.

喇叭套件公司 / 包装 / 高保真

顶级

真棒

放大器

Once we have developed the product structure, we can determine the number of units of each item required to satisfy demand for a new order of 50 Awesome speaker kits, as shown:

单位数量

Part B: 2 × number of As = 2 × 50 = 100

Part C: 3 × number of As = 3 × 50 = 150

Part D: 2 × number of Bs + 2 × number of Fs = 2 × 100 + 2 × 300 = 800

Part E: 2 × number of Bs + 2 × number of Cs = 2 × 100 + 2 × 150 = 500

Part F: 2 × number of Cs = 2 × 150 = 300

Part G: 1 × number of Fs = 1 × 300 = 300

Thus, for 50 units of A, we will need 100 units of B, 150 units of C, 800 units of D, 500 units of E, 300 units of F, and 300 units of G.

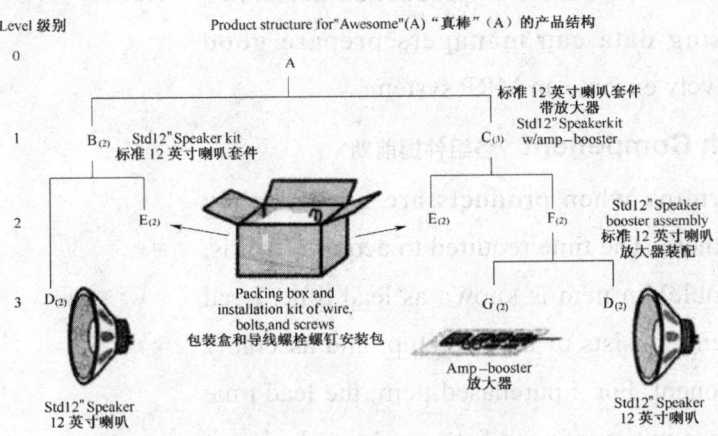

Fig. 13.3 Developing a product structure and requirements 开发产品结构和需求

2.3 Accurate Inventory Records 准确的库存记录

The inventory records file can be quite lengthy. The MRP program accesses the status segment of the record according to specific time periods (called time buckets in MRP slang). These records are accessed as needed during the program run. The MRP program performs its analysis from the top of the product structure downward, calculating requirements level by level. There are times, however, when it is desirable to identify the parent item that caused the material requirement. The MRP program allows the creation of a peg record file either separately or as part of the inventory record file. Pegging requirements allows us to retrace a material requirement upward in the product structure through each level, identifying each parent item that created the demand. Inventory transactions file is kept up to update by posting inventory transactions as they occur. These changes occur because of stock receipts and disbursements, scrap losses, wrong parts, canceled orders, and so forth.

2.4 Purchase Orders Outstanding 未完成的采购订单

Knowledge of outstanding orders should exist as a by-product of well-managed purchasing and inventory-control departments. When purchase orders are executed, records of those orders and their scheduled delivery dates must be available to production personnel. Only with good purchasing data can managers prepare good production plans and effectively execute an MRP system.

2.5 Lead Times for Each Component 各组件提前期

Once managers determine when products are needed, they determine when to acquire them. The time required to acquire (that is, purchase, produce, or assemble) an item is known as lead time. Lead time for a manufactured item consists of move, setup, and assembly or run times for each component. For a purchased item, the lead time includes the time between recognition of need for an order and when it is available for production in Fig. 13.4.

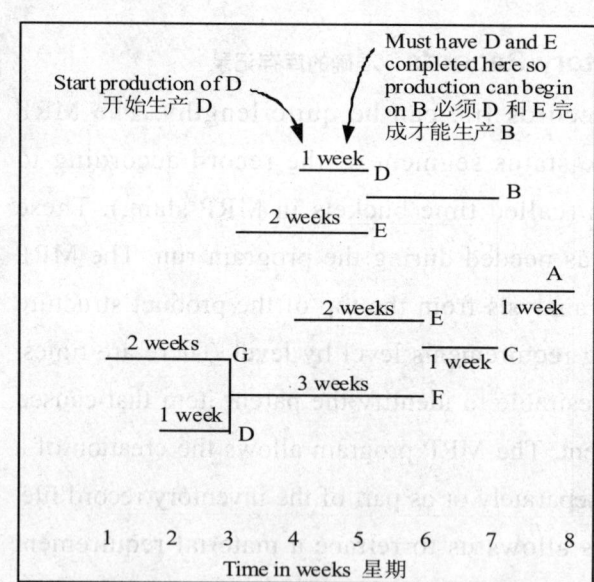

Fig. 13.4 Time-Phased Product Structure

3. MRP Structure MRP 结构

MRP requires information concerning independent demand, which comes from the master production schedule (MPS). The MPS contains gross requirements, the current inventory status known as on-hand inventory, and the status of outstanding orders. As with the previous product-speaker we can see its MRP structure in Table 13.1.   可用库存/未完成的

The basic MRP procedure is simple. We will discuss each of the steps in detail. But briefly, for each level in the bill of material, beginning with end items, MRP does the following for each part: (1) Netting: Determine net requirements by subtracting on-hand inventory and any scheduled receipts from the gross requirements. The gross requirements for level-zero items come from the MPS, while those for lower-level items are the result of previous MRP operations. (2) Lot sizing: Divide the net requirements into appropriate lot sizes to form jobs. (3) Time phasing: Offset the due dates of the jobs with lead times to determine start times. (4) BOM explosion: Use the start times, the lot sizes, and the BOM to generate gross requirements of any required components at the next level(s). (5) Iterate: Repeat these steps until all level are processed.   净需求/净需求量/减去 计划接收量

批量规则

时间分段/到期日 展开

迭代

Table 13.1 MRP Structure for Awesome Speaker   真棒喇叭 MRP 结构

Lot size 批量规则	Lead Time (weeks) 提前期	On Hand 可用库存	Level Code 级别代码	Item ID 产品标识		Week 周							
						1	2	3	4	5	6	7	8
Lot-for-Lot	1	10	0	A	Gross Requirements 总需求								50
					Scheduled Receipts 计划接收量								
					On-hand Inventory 可用库存量	10	10	10	10	10	10	10	10
					Net Requirements 净需求								40
					Planned Order Receipts 计划投入量								40
					Planned Order Releases 计划产出量							40	
Lot-for-Lot	2	15	1	B	Gross Requirements							80[A]	
					Scheduled Receipts								
					On-hand Inventory	15	15	15	15	15	15	15	
					Net Requirements							65	
					Planned Order Receipts							65	
					Planned Order Releases						65		

(续表)

Lot size 批量规则	Lead Time (weeks) 提前期	On Hand 可用库存	Level Code 级别代码	Item ID 产品标识		Week 周							
						1	2	3	4	5	6	7	8
Lot-for-Lot	1	20	1	C	Gross Requirements							120[A]	
					Scheduled Receipts								
					On-hand Inventory	20	20	20	20	20	20	20	20
					Net Requirements							100	
					Planned Order Receipts							100	
					Planned Order Releases						100		
Lot-for-Lot	2	10	2	E	Gross Requirements					130[B]	200[C]		
					Scheduled Receipts								
					On-hand Inventory	10	10	10	10	10	10		
					Net Requirements					120	200		
					Planned Order Receipts					120	200		
					Planned Order Releases			120	200				
Lot-for-Lot	3	5	2	F	Gross Requirements						200[C]		
					Scheduled Receipts								
					On-hand Inventory	5	5	5	5	5	5		
					Net Requirements						195		
					Planned Order Receipts						195		
					Planned Order Releases			195					
Lot-for-Lot	1	10	3	D	Gross Requirements			390[F]		130[B]			
					Scheduled Receipts								
					On-hand Inventory	10	10	10	10				
					Net Requirements			380		130			
					Planned Order Receipts			380		130			
					Planned Order Releases		380		130				
Lot-for-Lot	2	0	3	G	Gross Requirements			195[F]					
					Scheduled Receipts								
					On-hand Inventory			0					
					Net Requirements			195					
					Planned Order Receipts			195					
					Planned Order Releases	195							

*Note that the superscript is the source of the demand. 注：表中的上标表示需求来源。

4. Extensions of MRP MRP扩展

Recent years we have seen the development of a number of extensions of MRP. In this section, we review three of them.

4.1 Closed-loop MRP 闭环MRP

Closed-loop material requirements planning implies an MRP system that provides <u>feedback</u> to scheduling from the inventory 反馈

control system. Specifically, a closed-loop MRP system provides information to the capacity plan, master production schedule, and ultimately to the production plan. Virtually all commercial MRP systems are closed-loop. We can see its work flow in Fig. 13.5.

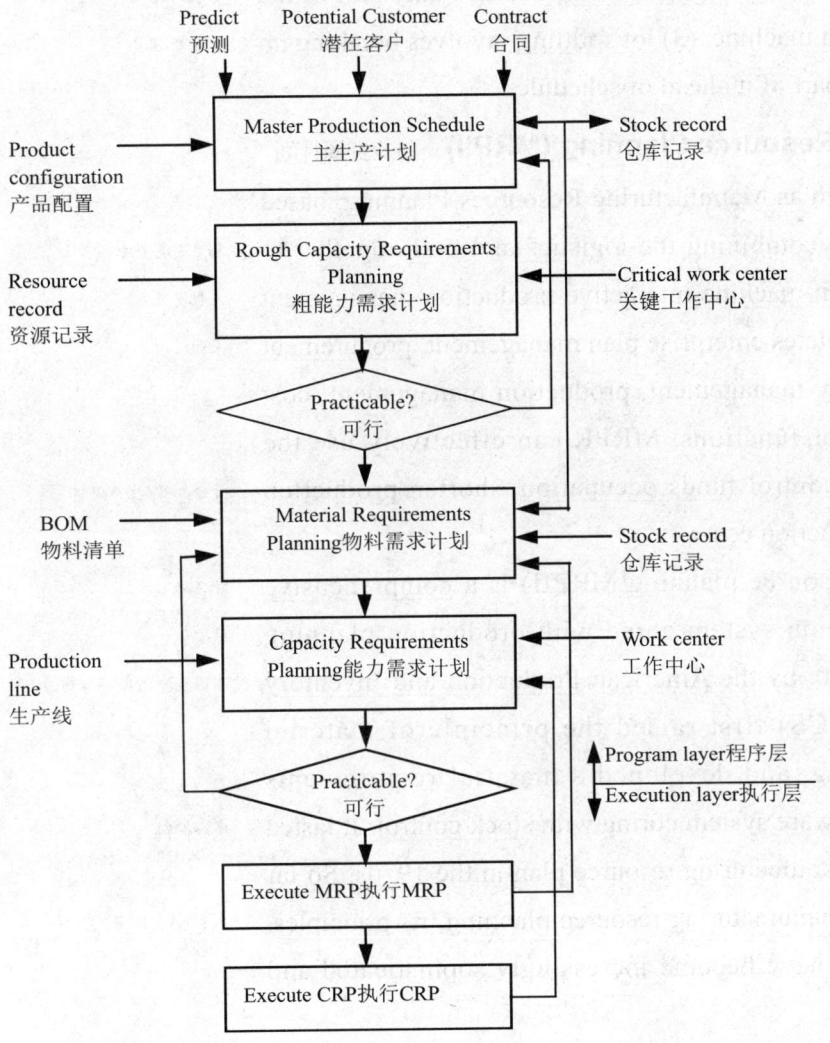

Fig. 13.5 The workflow of the closed-loop MRP

4.2 Capacity Requirements Planning 能力需求计划

In keeping with the definition of closed-loop MRP, feedback about workload is obtained from each work center. Load reports show the resource requirements in a work center for all work currently assigned to the work center, all work planned, and expected orders. Tactics for smoothing the load and minimizing the impact of changed lead time include the following: (1) <u>Overlapping</u>, which reduces the lead time, sends <u>pieces</u> to the second operation before the <u>entire lot</u> is completed on the first operation. (2) <u>Operations splitting</u> sends the lot to two different machines for the same operation. This involves an additional setup, but results in shorter <u>throughput times</u>, because only part of the lot is processed on each machine. (3) <u>lot splitting</u> involves breaking up the order and running part of it ahead of schedule.

重叠
工件 / 全部批量
操作拆分
吞吐时间
批量拆分

4.3 Manufacturing Resource Planning (MRPII) 制造资源计划

MRPII, also known as Manufacturing Resources Planning, based on closed-loop MRP, combining the <u>logistics</u> and <u>cash</u> together to form a complete <u>human-machine interactive</u> production management system. It mainly completes enterprise plan management, <u>procurement</u> management, inventory management, production management, cost management and other functions. MRPII can effectively use the enterprise resources, control <u>funds occupation</u>, shorten <u>production cycles</u> and reduce production costs.

物流 / 现金流
人机交互
采购
资金占用 / 生产周期

Manufacturing resource planning(MRPII) is a <u>comprehensive</u> management information system <u>cored</u> with production planning and control. From 1960, by the <u>American Production and Inventory Control Society(APICS)</u> first raised the principle of material requirements planning, and developed a material requirements planning computer software system coring with <u>stock control</u>. It lasted 30 years to form the manufacturing resource plan in the 1970s. So far the appearance of the manufacturing resource planning, its principles, methods and software have become increasingly sophisticated and perfectly.

综合的
核心
美国生产与库存控制协会
库存控制

专业词汇

material requirements planning(MRP)
物料需求计划
manufacturing resource planning(MRPII)
制造资源计划
bill of material(BOM) 物料清单
inventory 库存

job shop 车间
in stock 库存，有存货
transaction 交易
by-product 副产品
delivery date 交货期
gross requirement 总需求

inventory availability 库存量
master production schedule(MPS) 主生产计划
dependent demand 依赖需求
specifications 规范
lead times 提前期
standard hours 标准工时
financial plan 财务计划
labor availability 劳动力供应
inventory fluctuations 库存波动
supplier performance 供应商绩效
aggregate plan 总计划
time-phased plan 时间分段计划
end item 最终产品
subassembly 组件

on-hand inventory 可用库存
net requirement 净需求量
scheduled receipts 计划接收量
planned order receipts 计划投入量
planned order releases 计划产出量
lot sizing 批量规则
feedback 反馈
capacity plan 能力计划
workload 工作量
logistics 物流
procurement 采购
funds occupation 资金占用
production cycle 生产周期
stock control 库存控制

思考题：

1. 什么是物料需求计划（MRP）和制造资源计划（MRPII）？两者有何区别？
2. 什么是主生产计划（MPS）？主生产计划与总计划的区别与联系是什么？
3. 主生产计划有哪三种过程策略？请举例说明。
4. 在进行 MRP 的运算时，净需求是如何计算的？
5. 什么叫提前期？如何计算提前期？
6. 假如订单要求生产 100 个喇叭，请按照图 13.3 中喇叭的 BOM 结构计算各零部件的需求量。
7. 在表 13.1 中，假如喇叭的总需求量为 100，各部件的可用库存量均为 15，试重新编制该产品各部件的物料需求计划表。
8. 简述闭环 MRP 系统的工作流程。

Chapter 14　Enterprise Resource Planning
企业资源计划

1. Introduction　简介

ERP system is defined as a packaged software application that connects and manages information flows within and across a complex organization, allowing managers to make decisions based on information that truly reflects the current state of their activity. Today's ERP systems stem from Material Requirements Planning (MRP) and Manufacturing Resource Planning (MRPII). ERP is benefited to most of the organizations in reducing inventory, reducing manpower, improving productivity, increase in revenue, on time delivery and many more intangible benefits. Almost all large scale firms have either implemented or in process of implementing ERP. However, large firms are not only ones impacted by ERP systems, Small-and medium-sized firms also make extensive use of ERP systems.

打包的软件应用
信息流
复杂的
现状
起源于
有利的
库存/人力
生产力/收益/交货
无形的/大规模企业
实现
影响/中小企业
广泛地

2. The Function of ERP　ERP 的功能

Enterprise resources planning (ERP), which is based on the development of the computer and management technology, provides the whole solution to the management of the enterprise from the theory and practice aspects. ERP surpasses the traditional concept of the ERP, which absorbs the JIT, TQC and other management idea, expanding the management information system. The ERP system has the function of quantity management, decision support and other functions such as the function of finance, production management and human resources. Besides, the ERP supports the internet, intranet, extranet and E-business.

The objective of an ERP system is to coordinate a firm's whole business, from supplier evaluation to customer invoicing. This objective is seldom achieved, but ERP systems are evolving

解决方案
超越
及时生产/全面质量控制
管理信息系统
决策支持
财务/人力资源
另外/内联网/外联网
电子商务
协调
供应商/评估/发票
演变

as umbrella systems that tie together a variety of specialized systems. This is accomplished by using a centralized database to assist the flow of information among business functions. Exactly, what is tied together and how varies on a case-by-case basis are shown as Fig. 14.1.

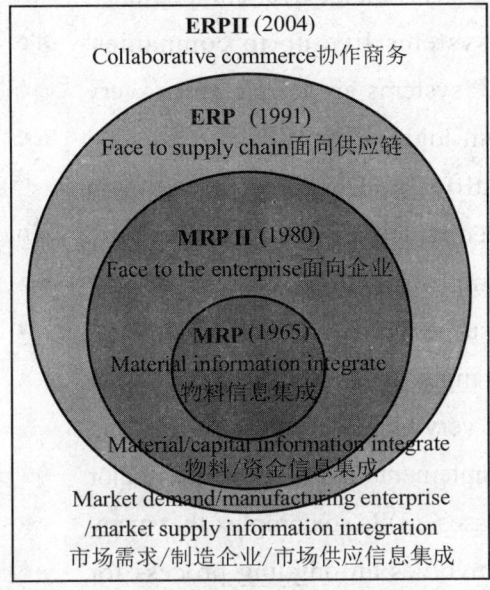

Fig. 14.1 Expansion Relationship between MRP and ERP

ERP usually is constituted by the six functions: (1) Automate and integrate many of their business process; (2) Share a common database throughout the enterprise; (3) Provide financial and human resource management information; (4) Provide modern logistics management systems; (5) Carry out the lean production system; (6) Exploit the new software (such as SCM and CRM).

3. Advantages and Disadvantages of ERP Systems
ERP 系统的优缺点

A global provider of market intelligence and advisory services for IT and consumer technology markets, International Data Corporations (IDC), found that global spending on ERP systems increased at an aggregate annual rate of 13.5% between 2001 and 2006, reaching $187 billion in 2006 while a later study anticipated a 5% annual growth from 2006 to 2010. We have alluded to some of the pluses of ERP. Here is a more complete list of advantages: (1) Provides integration of the supply-chain, and administrative process. (2) Creates commonality of databases. (3) Can incorporate improved and reengineered best processes. (4) Increases communication and collaboration among business partners and sites. (5) Has a software database that is off-the-shelf coding. (6) May provide a strategic advantage over competitors.

But in practice, not all ERP systems live up to companies' expectations due to the fact that ERP systems are too complex, very time-consuming, expensive, and own logic of workflow embedded in software packages. The difficulties and high failure rate in implementing ERP systems have been widely cited in the literature. Before 2000, about 90% of the ERP implementations were late or over budget and the ERP implementation success rate was only about 33%. We also have alluded to some of the minuses of ERP. Here is a more complete list of disadvantages: (1) Is very expensive to purchase, and even more costly to customize. (2) Implementation may require major changes in the company and its processes. (3) Is so complex that many companies cannot adjust to it. (4) Involves an ongoing process for implementation, which may never be completed. (5) Expertise in ERP is limited, with an ongoing problem.

4. The Key of ERP Implement ERP 实施的关键

In spite of ERP failures, Small and Medium Enterprises are witnessing increased pressure to improve efficiency, productivity, and competitiveness. Moreover, since some of the SMEs are working closely with large global enterprises, they are forced to adopt streamlined automated operations. The automation of the processes would enable them best to conduct business as part of an extended enterprise of large companies. Therefore, the assessment of ERP performance or benefits in ERP adopted companies is always an important challenge for decision makers and practitioners. So we have concluded some key success factors, such as: (1) Implement the ERP is to reform generally in management in the enterprise; (2) The leader of the enterprise should reach a consensus; (3) The devotion of the ERP is a systems engineering; (4) Implement the ERP needs interdisciplinary talent.

5. CASE: Managing Benetton with ERP Software
案例：用 ERP 软件管理 Benetton 公司

Thanks to ERP, the Italian sportswear company Benetton can probably claim to have the world's fastest factory. Located in Ponzano, Italy, Benetton makes and ships 50 million pieces of clothing each year. That is 30,000 boxes every day-boxes that must be filled with exactly the items ordered going to the correct store of the 5,000 Benetton outlets in 60 countries. This highly automated distribution center uses only 19 people. Without ERP, 400 people would be needed.

Here is how ERP software works: (1) Ordering. A salesperson in the south Boston store finds that she is running out of a best-selling blue sweater. Using a laptop PC, her local Benetton sales agent taps into the ERP sales module. (2) Availability. ERP's inventory software simultaneously forwards the order to the mainframe in Italy and finds that half the order can be filled immediately from the Italian warehouse. The rest will be manufactured and shipped in 4 weeks. (3) Production. Because the blue sweater was originally created by computer-aided design (CAD), ERP manufacturing software passes the specifications to a knitting machine. The knitting machine makes the sweaters. (4) Warehousing. The blue sweaters are boxed with a radio frequency ID (RFID) tag addressed to the Boston store and placed in one of the 300,000 slots in the Italian warehouse. A robot, by reading RFID tags, picks out any and all boxes ready for the Boston store, and loads them for shipment. (5) Order tracking. The Boston salesperson logs onto the ERP system through the Internet and sees that the sweaters (and other items) are completed and being shipped. (6) Planning. Based on data from ERP's forecasting and financial modules, Benetton's chief buyer decides that blue sweaters are in high demand and quite profitable. She decides to add three new hues.

sportswear	运动服装
outlets / distribution center	销售点 / 配送中心
Ordering	订购
running out of / best-selling	卖完 / 畅销的
sweater / laptop PC / taps into	运动服 / 笔记本电脑 / 接入
module / Availability	模块 / 可用性
simultaneously / forwards / mainframe	同时 / 转发 / 主机
warehouse / shipped	仓库 / 发货
Production	生产
specifications / knitting machine	规格 / 针织机
Warehousing / boxed / radio frequency ID (RFID) tag addressed to / slots	仓储 / 装箱 / 无线射频设别标签 / 地址为 / 货架
shipment / Order tracking	搬运 / 订单跟踪
logs onto	登录
forecasting	计划 / 预测
chief buyer	主要买家
profitable / hues	盈利的 / 色调

专业词汇

enterprise resources planning(ERP) 企业资源计划
manpower 人力
productivity 生产力
revenue 收益
small and medium-sized enterprises(SMEs) 中小企业
solution 解决方案
management information system(MIS) 管理信息系统
decision support 决策支持
finance 财务
human resources 人力资源
E-business 电子商务
supplier 供应商
centralized database 集中式数据库

business process 业务流程
provider 提供商
advisory 咨询
aggregate annual rate 综合年增长率
supply-chain 供应链
administrative process 管理流程
expectation 预期
workflow 工作流
budget 预算
competitiveness 竞争力
streamline 流水线
distribution center 配送中心
best-selling 畅销的
warehouse 仓库
radio frequency ID(RFID) tag 无线射频设别标签

思考题：

1. 简述 ERP 系统的定义以及它与 MRP 系统之间的区别与联系。
2. 在企业实施 ERP 系统带来的优点和缺点是什么？
3. ERP 系统在企业成功实施的关键是什么？

Chapter 15　Manufacturing Execution Systems
制造执行系统

1. Background　背景

Applying information technology to assist in the execution of production, through on-line management of the activities at the plant floor, has been a rapidly growing trend for a number of years. Planning systems have been applied under a variety of titles, including Material Requirements Planning(MRP), Manufacturing Resources Planning(MRPII), Enterprise Requirements Planning(ERP), and Manufacturing Control Systems(MCS). Also in place for many years are modern control systems that manage or control a machine's functions such as PLCs used to run machine tools. The Manufacturing Execution Systems(MES) bridges the gap between the planning system and the controlling system using on-line information to manage the current application of manufacturing resources: people, equipment and inventory. With direct electronic connections to the planning system and the equipment control systems, the MES is the hub that collects and provides information and direction within the production activities. To support on-line management decisions the MES usually includes direct connection to functions such as SPC, Time & Attendance, Product Data Management, Maintenance Management, and any other similar tool.

2. A General Overview　概述

2.1 Technology Evolves　技术发展

The idea of using computers to manage manufacturing activities is not new. The concepts that allowed the development of Materials Requirements Planning evolved from computer usage primarily within the accounting departments and were extensions of tools used for cost accounting and inventory measurement. Even the systems used by manufacturing have been oriented toward accounting and finance. This appears to be part of the reason for the distance between many manufacturing professionals and true computer implementation on the manufacturing floor. Many legitimate complaints are often stated about the computer systems used in manufacturing. For example: The information is too old, I need to make decisions based on what is happening now.

A new idea is evolving. In recent years a concept with many versions has been developed for manufacturing managers – a real tool that helps manage the manufacturing floor, functions, resources, and inventory and gives accounting and MIS all the information they require. The best part is this idea is being built around the manufacturing world and requires no advanced knowledge of computers. In most cases these systems run on smaller local computers and are fairly simple to use.

2.2 Manufacturing Execution Systems 制造执行系统

This concept has been around long enough to have a name: Manufacturing Execution Systems (MES). As the name implies, MES is more than a planning tool like ERP or MRPII. MES is an on-line extension of the planning system with an emphasis on execution or carrying out the plan. Execution means include: (1) Making products, (2) Making and measuring parts, (3) Changing order priorities, (4) Assigning and reassigning personnel, (5) Scheduling and rescheduling equipment, (6) Turning machines on and off, (7) Moving inventory to/from work stations, (8) Setting and reading measuring controls, (9) Assigning and reassigning inventory.

2.3 Manufacturing Execution Tool 制造执行工具

The MES is a manufacturing tool designed and built for manufacturing. Most manufacturing companies use a planning process (MRPII/ERP or equivalent) to determine what products are to be manufactured. Once that plan has been developed, there must be a translation of the plan that deals with real resources that are currently available. What is necessary is a method to take input from the planning system and translate that plan into a language that fits the plant floor and the resources required to execute the plan.

2.4 What MES Can Do for You MES 能为你做什么

International MESA has conducted studies of companies using MES and offers the following benefits as reported by system users: reduces manufacturing cycle time, reduces work-in-process inventory, reduces paperwork between shifts, eliminates lost blueprints, improves customer service, reduces or eliminates data entry time, reduces lead times, improves product quality, empowers plant operations people, responds to unanticipated events.

The potential gain by implementing MES addresses the need for immediate, current, on-line information that allows users to make the best informed decisions regarding the application of inventory, plant resources, and people. Some examples include: (1) Engineering wants to locate all current work orders for a given product to determine the effect of an immediate engineering change. (2) Some purchased material that is specific to a given customer's order currently in process has arrived as a partial shipment, 72% complete. Where is the order and what is the appropriate response? (3) A customer requires specific operator information including operator, date, and ambient conditions to be supplied with each item produced. (4) A process critical to production needs preventative maintenance. How are the current orders to be scheduled? (5) The president of a high-volume customer has just called and needs to know by tomorrow if he can double the quantity on the current order in house without affecting the delivery schedule. (6) There are 26 work orders totaling 443 hours of work for a specific routing location. What is the optimum sequence for these work orders and what factors should be considered? (7) A new quality assurance system has been installed that can receive and analyze data from the plant floor and provide current on-line results to the workstation operator. (8) Operator time is charged to each order and collected through the use of bar code readers. (9) Inventory can be retrieved from storage and sent to a specific workstation matching the production schedule. (10) The shift supervisor is considering replacing a part on a production machine and needs to know if the part is <u>in stock</u> and how long the maintenance work will take. (11) Information regarding <u>inbound inventory</u> can be gained by a communication link with the <u>vendor's</u> MES computer. (12) A <u>sales representative</u> is at a customer's office and needs to know where their order is in the production process.

3. MES Core Functions MES 核心功能

Fig. 15.1 is an overview of the core functions of the MES.

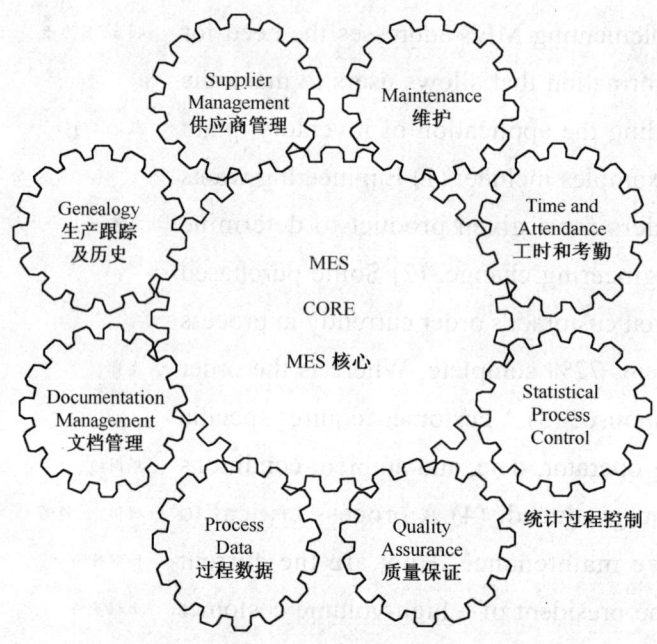

Fig. 15.1 Core Functions of MES

3.1 Planning System Interface 计划系统接口

The MES should be directly <u>coupled to</u> the planning system to accept work orders and all other input and to provide upload information as necessary. The communications should be two way so the MES can keep the planning system properly informed about <u>plant</u> activities such as <u>labor</u> data, inventory changes, and work order progress. Other methods of <u>data entry</u> and reporting can easily be <u>accommodated</u>, and in some cases, such as more continuous process, production orders may not be used at all.

3.2 Work Orders 工单

The MES accepts the Work Order through automatic or manual entry. It manages changes on orders, establishes and changes schedules, and maintains a prioritized sequenced plan. Releasing orders to production and establishing a current order priority list based on your sequencing rules is a normal part of MES. Frequently changes must be made to release orders. Within MES, order modifications such as these examples can be done easily: enter schedule changes, mark for material shortage, enter quantity changes, split orders or combine orders. The Work Order management function maintains a constant real time view of the work orders in the current backlog and the status of each order.

手工的
优先的
优先级列表
排序规则
修改
标记
拆分 / 合并
积压

3.3 Work Stations 工作站

This part of the system is responsible for implementing the direction of the Work Order plan and the logical configuration of the Work Stations. The planning, scheduling, and loading of each operational Work Station is done here, providing the current and total shop load by operation using routing data and time standards. Based on this plan, the system will request and manage delivery of inventory, tooling, and data in response to the Bill of Material requirements and will issue and execute commands to move the required items to the planned Work Station. The MES can and should include the direct control interface and connection with each Work Station.

配置
计划 / 调度
车间负载
工装
分发
接口

3.4 Inventory Tracking and Management 库存追踪与管理

While the planning system has the aggregate data on inventory, the detail can easily reside at the local level MES. "Dock To Stock" operations are accomplished here with regular updates to the planning system. A current map of all inventory and storage locations, including WIP, is maintained.

总数据
驻留 / 码头到仓库
完成
在制品

3.5 Material Movement 物料转移

Another major area of MES system contribution is the movement of inventory or information to the needed location on the plant floor.

This portion of the system controls material movement in the plant, in manual or automatic systems, by issuing requests for a manual move or issuing commands to material handling system, such as AGV, conveyor systems, carrousels, robots, etc. The commands can be as simple as "move this item from this location to that location." Data Collection is the eyes and ears for management and gathers information. Through various kinds of sensing devices and control interfaces, data from the floor operations can be collected, collated, and dispersed on whatever basis is desired. This is the primary method for all personnel to communicate with the MES, either through information input/output by system operators or recognition of events electronically. Direct connections with PLCs to collect information are also part of this function area.

部分
自动导引小车
传送／装运转盘

数据采集
传感设备
接口／整理
分散

识别

3.6 Exception Management 异常管理

The most custom portion of the MES is addressing how a company responds to plan exceptions. What happens when a Work Station is suddenly down, or when material is not available, or when a Work Order becomes "hot"? The MES should be able to take these changes in stride and respond with alternative actions. Our process began with a planned or sequenced list of Work Orders, methods to schedule those Work Orders into Work Stations, control of inventory assignment, and management of material movement. Along with data collection to keep the system current and a way to handle exceptions, we have the ability to execute the manufacturing plan.

定制的／致力于

不影响正常活动地／可替代的

分配

4. Support Functions 支持功能

Other components of Manufacturing Execution Systems act as support functions. These are programs or software packages that support manufacturing but are not part of the planning process or the device control system. The most popular applications are listed here, but there are others, and more will be developed in the future: (1) Statistical Process Control, (2)Maintenance Management, (3) Time and Attendance, (4)Product Data Management, (5) Process Data/ Performance Analysis, (6) Supplier Management, (7) Genealogy/

部分
软件

统计过程控制

性能分析／历史

Product Traceability, (8) Laboratory Information Management, (9) Quality Assurance.

5. System Requirements 系统要求

MES projects have developed on a somewhat piecemeal basis, but as the concept grows, the need for broader system design considerations for all software and hardware is increasingly obvious. Major system revisions as well as all new systems should be designed to include:

(1) Full Integration. All systems must be able to exchange information and not be excluded from the overall system process. The concept of the information warehouse where each computerized activity draws from and delivers data to the system is becoming increasingly important.

(2) Scalability To Future Needs. The design of the software and hardware must allow upward scalability to meet the increasing needs of your company as growth and change occurs.

(3) Compatibility With Existing Systems. Ideally, an MES system should be incorporated into the existing systems. However, this may not be economically feasible with systems using older software.

(4) Broad System Access. Information is the tool that gives users access to what is going on. It will be increasingly more important to broaden the audience of information users. Do not be overly restrictive.

(5) Security. While broad access is a cornerstone, so too is the requirement of adequate security, primarily to ensure data integrity.

6. Application Examples 应用案例

6.1 Planning System Data Exchange 计划系统数据交换

A major role of the MES is to collect, collate, and upload data to the planning level system. It would be difficult to describe each possible scenario since there are many existing and available varieties of planning system installations and products. Each system interface must stand on its own depending on the input and output requirements.

These requirements can best be established in a meeting with the planning system vendor, the users, and the MES provider. This meeting should be held early in the system design process to determine the feasibility of the interface.

6.2 Receiving Within MES 在 MES 内接收

Receiving can be treated as another group of work stations with processing routings established by reading the bar code label (either PO number or part number). This displays a screen to the receiving personnel for appropriate data entry and establishes the routing for this specific receipt. At this point, the material begins its tracking within the inventory function and is directed through quality assurance processing steps. The material may be sent to a buffer storage area for later retrieval and assignment to a specific processing work station. Following the processing steps, the material can be put into inventory for assignment to production orders, is sent to the appropriate Work Station for disposition. Disposition decisions are made and executed with status inputs to the MES and uploaded to the purchasing and inventory modules of the planning system.

6.3 Timed Operation Routing 定时操作路线

The MES can automatically perform timed operations as part of the routing used in Work Station scheduling. An example of a timed operation might be a "burn in" operation where the product is removed from a Work Station, sent to storage, and retrieved automatically after the timed function is complete.

6.4 Work Scheduling or Sequencing 工作调度与排序

A very obvious question that should be asked frequently in manufacturing management is "What is the schedule of work to be performed?" Though it may seem obvious or intuitive, the area of schedule development probably offers the best opportunity for improving the resource management process. The issue here is not to determine production quantities (that was determined by the planning system), but rather how to rank a given list of tasks based on the resources (people, equipment, and inventory) currently available.

专业词汇

- manufacturing execution systems(MES) 制造执行系统
- plant floor 工厂车间
- PLC 可编程逻辑控制器
- attendance 考勤
- cost accounting 成本会计
- manufacturing cycle time 生产周期
- work-in-process(WIP) 在制品
- blueprints 蓝图
- work order 工单
- delivery schedule 交付时间表
- bar code reader 条码阅读器
- retrieve 检索
- shift supervisor 值班主任
- sales representative 销售代表
- sequencing rule 排序规则
- configuration 配置
- scheduling 调度
- AGV 自动导引小车
- data collection 数据采集
- sensing device 传感设备
- scalability 可伸缩性
- compatibility 兼容性
- data integrity 数据完整性
- feasibility 可行性
- vendor 提供商

思考题：

1. 什么是制造执行系统？它与 MRP 或 ERP 等计划系统的区别与联系是什么？
2. MES 的主要功能有哪些？
3. 举例说明 MES 在工厂车间的用途。
4. 在 MES 中有哪些信息需要实现与计划系统的集成？

Part IV

Advanced Manufacturing Mode

先进制造模式

Chapter 16   Lean Production
精益生产

1. The Origin of Lean Production   精益生产的起源

Lean production or <u>lean thinking</u> has its <u>origin</u> in the <u>philosophy</u> of achieving improvements in most economical ways with special focus on reducing <u>muda</u>. The concept of muda became one of the most important concepts in quality improvement activities primarily originated by <u>Taiichi Ohno's</u> famous production philosophy from Toyota in the early 1950s. This philosophy was widely called as <u>Toyota production system</u> in Japan, and it became later on labeled as lean production and lean thinking by <u>Womack</u> et al..

| 精益思想 / 起源 / 理念
| 浪费
| 大野耐一
| 丰田生产系统
| 沃麦克

Toyota adopted <u>statistical</u> quality control methods in the last part of 1949 by attending the statistical quality control course provided by <u>JUSE</u> to overcome the crisis. At the same time <u>Eiji Toyoda</u> went to USA to study how <u>automobiles</u> were manufactured in the world's largest and most efficient manufacturing <u>plant</u> – Ford's Rough plant in <u>Detroit</u>. At that time, Ford's Rough plant produced 7,000 cars per day, which seemed like a dream compared to Toyota's accumulated results of 13 years of effort by 1950 – 2685 cars. It is understandable, that Eiji Toyoda decided to study <u>intensively</u> how cars were produced in this plant.

| 统计
| 日本科学技术联盟 / 丰田英二
| 汽车
| 工厂
| 底特律
| 深入

During his stay at Ford Eiji wrote back to the <u>headquarter</u>, that he "thought there were some possibilities to improve the production system" and back in Japan, Eiji and his production <u>genius</u>, Taiichi Ohno (who also visited Detroit several times), however soon concluded, that <u>mass production</u> as running at Ford could never work in Japan.

| 总部
| 天才
| 大批量生产

What they realised in USA was, that there was too much waste everywhere. There were wasted man power, efforts, materials, space and time, i.e. muda of man power, muda of production, muda of <u>inventories</u> and excess processing, muda of <u>defects</u>, muda of waiting,

| 库存 / 残次品

muda of transport, muda of facilities. For instance, they could observe that none of the specialists beyond the assembly worker were actually carrying out value adding activities to the production. They were just responsible for designing the production process and giving orders and instructions to the workers. The only activity of a foreman was to ensure, that line workers followed orders, and the assembly-line workers would just, repetitively, perform one or two simple tasks. From these observations they realised that they (Japan and Toyota) were too poor to have these kinds of waste (both of human resources and material resources), and they could not afford to just copy and implement, what they have seen in USA.

What Ohno did, when he returned to Japan, was firstly to establish groups with workers, and to encourage them to work together to perform the best way of operations. This first step was followed by the next step, where Ohno extended tasks for the teams to include tool repair, quality-checking, and other housekeeping jobs such as the five-S activities. When the teams were running well, Ohno extended further their tasks. Now he set time aside periodically for the team to suggest ways collectively to improve the process. This teamwork was the early version of "quality circles".

Another famous system to reduce muda (waste) was also invented by Ohno – the so-called just-in-time (JIT) or Kanban system. Ohno saw at Ford Detroit, how much muda was produced under the mass production system. For instance, there was high inventory cost to keep a large number of parts that were later found to be defective, when installed at the assembly plant. From this observation, Ohno developed a new way to co-ordinate the flow of parts within the supply system on a day-to-day basis, thus the parts would only be produced at each previous step to supply the immediate demand of the next step. This JIT system later on became much more efficient, when they used a kind of card (Kanban) as a tool for information exchange between different production lines. From that time, the JIT system was called as the Kanban system. In fact, Taiichi Ohno got this JIT idea, when he saw the modern supermarket system in USA.

By implementing JIT or Kanban system much muda could

be reduced. First of all, a large space was not necessary to keep a large number of parts. Second, only the needed quantity of parts was produced. Third, if defects were produced, it was immediately discovered, thus the system prevented a large number of defects to be produced. However, this new system was not easy to implement, especially if the system often produced defects. That means if just one small part of the whole production system failed with defects, the entire production system should be stopped. In fact, this point was precisely, what Ohno had thought about. He wanted that every member of the entire production system paid attention to the prevention of potential problems and in this way reduced muda.

In spite of several advantages of Ohno's new production system, his idea did not get popularity in the company. The majority of people were more interested in establishing the mass production facilities, and <u>thereby</u> to secure the production in quantity. Thus, Ohno's idea was in the beginning limited to be applied only in his own plant.

Focusing on quantity in production, Toyota increased <u>radically productivity</u>, and in 1959, Toyota produced for the first time 100,000 cars a year. However, Toyota was confronted with a serious <u>crisis</u> in the last part of the 1950s, when the US market rejected Toyota's new <u>brand Crown</u> for several reasons such as lack of security, lack of power, too heavy, etc. At the same time, the Japanese government was forced to <u>liberalize trade</u> by confronting pressures from overseas.

To improve quality was the <u>critical</u> factor in order to overcome the crisis. In this critical situation, the management team of Toyota agreed to implement <u>TQC</u> in the whole company together with the Kanban system. As a consequence of these activities and the improved quality, Toyota was awarded with the <u>Deming Prize</u>.

We know today that the Toyota Production System became so competitive that Toyota and other Japanese car manufacturers gradually increased their market shares all over the world. But it is important to remember that the so-called Toyota Production System was not a traditional quality <u>assurance</u> system as, e.g. an ISO9000-based quality system. It was first of all a human-based system where people were involved with continuous improvements, and the foundation for the system was leadership and empowerment through education and training.

2. The "Birth" of The Term "Lean Production"
精益生产术语的产生

The IMVP Researcher John Krafcik originally coined the term "lean production". IMPV is an abbreviation of the International Motor Vehicle Program established at Massachusetts Institute of Technology in 1985. During the following 5 years, the IMVP staff carried out the world's most comprehensive benchmarking study ever seen. The study collected data from automobile assembly plants all over the world in order to understand the differences in quality and productivity. The results of this benchmarking study were published in the well-known book The Machine that Changed the World (Womack et al., 1990), in which there is an exciting historical analysis of the machine called "the automobile". In the book, the origins and elements of lean production are presented together with the results of the benchmarking study.

We can conclude that the term "lean production" is a result of the benchmarking results from the IMVP. The word "lean" was suggested because the best assembly plants (the Japanese plants) in the study: Uses less of everything compared with mass production – half the human efforts in the factory, half the manufacturing space, half the investments in tools, half the engineering hours to develop a new product in half the time. Also it requires keeping far less than half the needed inventory on site, results in many fewer defects, and produces a greater and ever growing variety of products.

These impressive results have been achieved by the leading Japanese companies because of a continuous quest for quality improvements since 1950. We can say that the results are due to the quality evolution in Japan from 1950 to 1980 in which period most Western companies did not bother very much on quality issues. The new management philosophy "TQM" was borne in the last part of the 1980s partly because the West woke up and began to study "what happened in Japan".

3. Lean Production, Quality Management and Waste
精益生产，质量管理与浪费

TQM is a company culture characterized by increased customer satisfaction through continuous improvements, in which all employees actively participate. By comparing this definition of TQM with the ultimate objectives of the lean producers as described above it is obvious that there do not seem to be any contradictions between the two objectives. This is not a coincidence because the roots of TQM can be traced back to the Japanese quality evolution, where Toyota was one of the pioneering companies. Toyota practiced the philosophy and principles of TQC so early as in the last part of the 1950s. The Japanese version of TQC became later in the last part of the 1980s the main reference when the term TQM was born.

It is also not a coincidence that TQM was not mentioned at all in the first book about lean production The Machine that Changed the World. This book was published in 1990 and written in the last part of the 1980s, and TQM was not a well-known management philosophy at that time. The authors probably did not want to adopt the well-established Japanese term TQC – the forerunner of TQM. In the next book on lean production – Lean Thinking – several references to TQM have been included, but the authors did not discuss the similarities and differences to the key principles of TQM.

In the book Lean Thinking, the very first word is interestingly the Japanese word for waste (muda), and it is concluded that muda is everywhere. This is a very important observation not only in relation to lean production but also to TQM. By defining waste as the excess resources used compared with perfection we can say that the aim or objective of lean production is to eliminate waste. What then constitutes waste? In order to be able to work with a generic definition we suggest the following definition of waste: Waste is everything that increases cost without adding value for the customer. It was documented in the book The Machine that Changed the World that wastes can add up to very significant resources. The problem with waste is that you will not have an overview of its size because it is never registered or measured as a whole in the company's management accounting system. Some bits and pieces are measured and registered but most of it is invisible for the managers unless you compare your company's processes and cost structure with other companies. This comparison is called benchmarking.

Juran, who was one of the experts on quality control invited to Japan in 1954, was may be the first to deal with the different forms of waste. Since, then identification and reduction of waste has become one of the core activities of quality management. Juran called wastage for "the gold in the mine" or "quality costs" and later he called it "the cost of poor quality (COPQ)". In relation to waste and lean production it is interesting to compare Juran's definition from 1951 to his 1989 definition: (1) 1951. Quality costs – the costs which would disappear if no defects where produced. (2) 1989. The COPQ – is the sum of all costs that would disappear if there were no quality problems. Comparing these two definitions we should understand that in 1951 quality control was regarded as a narrow engineering discipline and the main activities were focused on defects in production. In 1988, quality control had developed into a holistic management philosophy called TQM, which was not only dealing with production but also all other processes in the company and all types of industries including services of any kind. By using the metaphor "the gold in the mine" Juran signalled that the size of quality costs could be of a significant size.

An example from a leading Danish service company indicates that the COPQ or waste is still "a problem everywhere". The example is from 1999 where one of the company's key processes was analysed in order to identify waste for improvements. The yearly salaries for running the process were calculated to approximately DKK 25 millions. As shown in Table 16.1, 74 percent of the total salaries were used on waste of different kinds! The waste related to production and correction of failures was 45 percent of the yearly salary! With an overlap of 16 percent with waste for failures the table shows that the waste for non-value adding activities was 46 percent! There was definitely a huge need for understanding and mastering the key principles for identifying and reducing waste in this company – and it is our experience that the need is everywhere – in any company – big, medium and small companies – public as well as private!

Table 16.1 A calculation of yearly salary costs used for waste

	Value adding activities 价值增加活动	Non-value adding activities 非价值增加活动
Failure free process 无故障过程	6.5 million (26 percent) (value adding costs – i.e. necessary costs)	7.5 million (30 percent) (non-value adding costs in failure free processes)
Production and correction of failures 生产和错误更正	7.2 million (29 percent) (costs for rectification of damages/failures 改正损失和故障的成本)	3.9 million (16 percent) (costs for producing and handling failures 生产和处理故障的成本)

4. The Principles of Lean Production 精益生产原则

The following five principles for reducing waste and building lean enterprises were given by Womack and Jones after about 6 years of thinking following the publication of the book The Machine that Changed the World in 1990: (1) specify value by specific product; (2) identify the value stream for each product; (3) make the value flow without interruptions; (4) let the customer pull value from the producer; (5) pursue perfection.

Some comments on the above principles will be given in the following. The first comment to the above five principles is that these principles were exactly the same as the ones, which were the guiding principles of craft production before mass production became the leading production philosophy in the industrialized nations. We can say that lean production is a production philosophy, which tries to combine the principles of craftsmanship with mass production. In craft production, the customer and his needs are in the focus, and no production will be initiated unless you have an order from a specific customer. When the order comes in all employees in the workshop works with commitment to satisfy the customer's needs. Everybody understands what the consequences with waste are for the customer, for the owner and for themselves. The employees understood the purpose of their work and they had pride in producing the products with the quality standard, which characterized the craftsmen of the workshop. These good attributes of craft production became lost in mass production with huge invisible waste as a consequence including the waste of not utilizing the brainpower of millions of workers all over the world. 　　利用 / 脑力

　　The second comment is that the five principles resemble very much the well-known quality improvement process developed by Motorola in the period 1983 to 1989. Motorola called the process for "the six steps to six sigma" – a process which helped Motorola to save billions of dollars. In fact, the six sigma methodology was first introduced in the USA in 1985 at Florida Power and Light (FPL) when the company decided to apply for the Deming Prize. FPL learned the six sigma methodology from the JUSE counsellors who helped FPL to prepare for the prize application. Motorola's six sigma process was developed and implemented first in manufacturing, and from 1990 the process was adapted to the non-manufacturing areas of the company.

像

六西格玛

弗罗里达电力照明公司

六西格玛质量管理方法 / 日本科学技术连盟 / 顾问

专业词汇

lean production(LP) 精益生产
Toyota production system 丰田生产系统
Taiichi Ohno
大野耐一（著名的丰田生产方式创始人）
muda（日语）浪费
statistical 统计
automobile 汽车
headquarter 总部
investment 投资
James P. Womack
詹姆斯·沃麦克（《精益思想》一书的作者）
JUSE 日本科学技术连盟
Eiji Toyoda 丰田英二（丰田汽车公司社长）
defects 残次品
assembly-line 装配线
just-in-time (JIT) 及时生产
Kanban system 看板系统

liberalize trade 自由贸易
TQC(total quality control)
全面质量控制
TQM(total quality management)
全面质量管理
Deming Prize 戴明奖（日本科学技术联盟颁发的质量管理奖）
benchmarking 标杆管理
The Machine that Changed the World
改变世界的机器（书名）
COPQ(cost of poor quality)
不良质量成本
DKK 丹麦克朗
industrialized nations 工业化国家
six sigma methodology
六西格玛质量管理方法

思考题：

1. 什么是精益生产？其核心思想是什么？
2. 什么是浪费？生产中有哪些形式的浪费？
3. 简述全面质量管理的内容。
4. 何谓标杆管理？
5. 简述精益生产的原则。

Chapter 17 Agile Manufacturing
敏捷制造

1. Agile Manufacturing-definitions 敏捷制造的定义

Agile manufacturing(AM) is a business concept that integrates organizations, people and technology into a meaningful unit by deploying advanced information technologies and flexible and nimble organization structures to support highly skilled, knowledgeable and motivated people. 'Lean' implies high productivity and quality, but it does not necessarily imply being responsive. 'Agile', on the other hand, stresses the importance of being highly responsive to meet the 'total needs' of the customer, while simultaneously striving to be lean – manufacturer whose primary goal is to be lean compromises responsiveness over cost-efficiencies. Agile manufacturers place equal importance on both cost and responsiveness.

Agile manufacturing can be said to be a relatively new, post-mass-production concept for the creation and distribution of goods and services. It is the ability to thrive in a competitive environment of continuous and unanticipated change and to respond quickly to rapidly changing markets driven by customer-based valuing of products and services. It includes rapid product realization, highly flexible manufacturing, and distributed enterprise integration. Technology alone does not make an agile enterprise. Companies should find the right combination of strategies, culture, business practices, and technology that are necessary to make it agile, taking into account the market characteristics.

Agile manufacturing is driven by the need to respond quickly to changing customer requirements. It demands a manufacturing system that is able to produce effectively a large variety of products and to be reconfigurable to accommodate changes in the product mix and product designs. Manufacturing system reconfigurability and product variety are critical aspects of agile manufacturing. The concept of agility has an impact on the design of assemblies. To implement agile manufacturing, methodologies for the design of agile manufacturing are needed. Design for agile assembly is accomplished by considering the operational issues of assembly systems at the early product design stage.

The manufacturing industry, particularly the One-of-a-Kind Product(OKP) industry, tends to be lean, agile and global. This tendency leads to a new concept of a virtual company that consists of several subproduction units geographically dispersed in the world as branches, joint ventures and subcontractors. Many OKP companies, such as those in shipbuilding have become virtual companies. For these virtual companies, traditional production control and management systems, methods and theories do not satisfy their needs for production planning and control. For some companies, therefore, there is a need to be transformed into a Virtual Enterprise(VE) in order to become agile. However, selecting partners based on flexibility and responsiveness alone will not lead to a reduction in cost and an improvement in the quality of products and services. A much wider spectrum of factors needs to be taken into account.

Agile manufacturing is an expression that is used to represent the ability of a producer of goods and services. The changes needed for agile manufacturers to thrive in the face of continuous change can occur in markets, in technologies, in business relationships and in all facets of the business enterprise. Such changes are not about small-scale continuous improvements, but an entirely different way of doing business. Agile manufacturing requires one to meet the changing market requirements by suitable alliances based on core-complementary competencies, organizing to manage change and uncertainty, and leveraging people and information.

The analysis of various definitions and concepts of AM show that all these definitions are polarized in a similar direction. Most definitions and concepts seem to highlight flexibility and responsiveness as well as virtual enterprises and information technologies. However, the question is whether one can achieve agility with minimum investment in technologies and processes. Hence, there is a need to redefine the definition of agility within this context. Fig. 17.1 presents the new model for explaining the agile manufacturing paradigm. The model takes into account the characteristics of the market, infrastructure, technologies and strategies. Its purpose is to highlight the new dimension of the definition of the agile manufacturing paradigm.

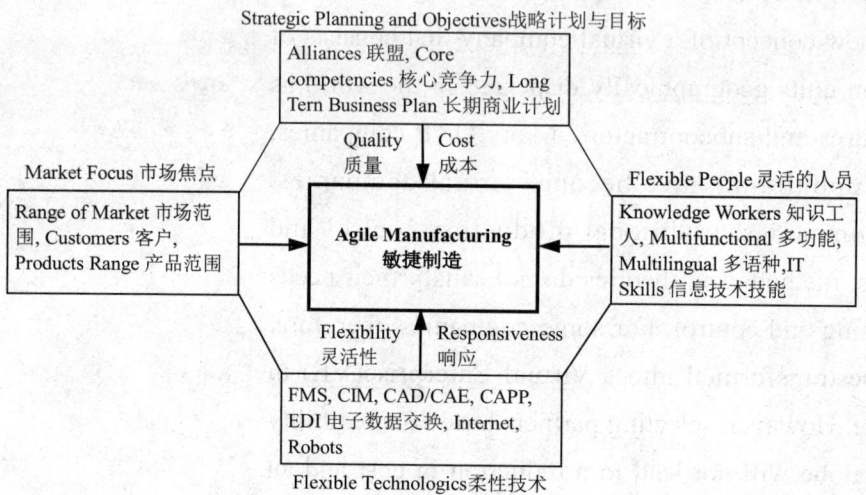

Fig. 17.1 Agile manufacturing paradigm

Based on some of these observations, Agility in manufacturing may be defined as: The capability of an organization, by proactively establishing virtual manufacturing with an efficient product development system, to (i) meet the changing market requirements, (ii) maximize customer service level and (iii) minimize the cost of goods, with an objective of being competitive in a global market and for an increased chance of long-term survival and profit potential. This must be supported by flexible people, processes and technologies.

2. Agile Manufacturing Strategies and Technologies
敏捷制造策略和技术

Analysing the overall characteristics of strategies and technologies, the literature available on AM can be grouped under the following themes: (i) strategic planning, (ii) product design, (iii) virtual enterprise and (iv) automation and Information Technology (IT). The details of the classification are illustrated in Fig. 17.2.

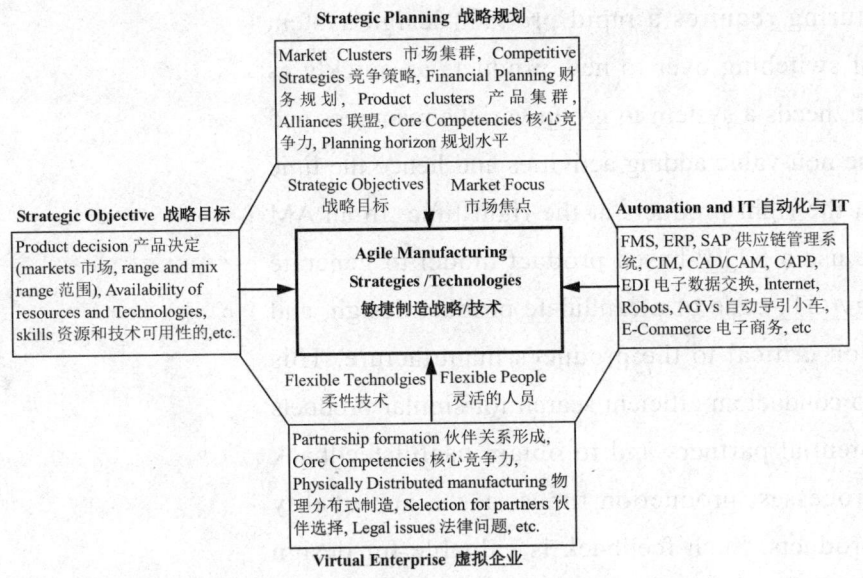

Fig. 17.2 Agile Manufacturing Strategies/Techniques

2.1 Strategic Planning 策略计划

Strategic planning of performance improvement is gaining attention in all areas of manufacturing. The reason for this is that it takes into account the long-term interest of the company in determining suitable business and operational policies. To achieve agility in manufacturing, several sub-strategies are needed, including virtual enterprise, rapid-partnership formation, rapid prototyping, and temporary alliances based on core competencies. Without suitable business and operations strategies, technologies and systems alone are not sufficient to achieve agility. Agile manufacturing can be achieved through customer-integrated multidisciplinary teams, supply chain partners, flexible manufacturing, computer-integrated information systems, and modular production facilities.

2.2 Product Design 产品设计

The agile manufacturing system should be able to produce a variety of components at low cost and in a short time period. People formulated a design for agility rule. The design rule reduces manufacturing lead times in consecutive changes of product models. Along with changes of product models, machines are relocated considering the overall costs of material handling and reconfiguration.

Agile manufacturing requires a rapid product design system with the objective of switching over to new products as quickly as possible. This, in turn, needs a system to group various resources and products to reduce the non-value adding activities and hence the time to reach market with the right products at the right time. In an AM environment, people use a STEP-based product model to generate the Group Technology(GT) code of a candidate product design, and additional information critical to the product's manufacture. This information is used to conduct an efficient search for similar products manufactured by potential partners and to obtain useful feedback on manufacturing processes, production times, costs, and quality attributes of these products. Such feedback is valuable for design evaluation and improvement early in the design cycle of a product in AM.

2.3 Virtual Enterprise 虚拟企业

A virtual organization is the integration of complementary core competencies distributed among a number of carefully chosen, but real organizations all with similar supply chains focusing on speed to market, cost reduction and quality. Generally, a single organization often may not be able to respond quickly to changing market requirements. Temporary alliances or partnerships based on core competencies of firms will help to improve the flexibility and responsiveness of organizations. However, coordination and integration could be complicated. Appropriate strategies and meth-odology, which will involve communication, training and education, and goal deployment, must be adopted for an effective coordination and integration of participating firms at different levels of cooperation.

Virtual Manufacturing(VM) is an integrated synthetic-manufacturing environment used to enhance all levels of decision and control in a manufacturing enterprise. The agile enterprise requires VM to respond to changing market requirements quickly. VM environments are being proposed to improve responsiveness, improve product and process design, reduce manufacturing risks, improve manufacturing design and operation, support manufacturing system changes, enhance product service and repair, increase manufacturing understanding, and provide a vehicle for manufacturing training and research. The VE environment places a number of special requirements on the process design activity. Since virtual enterprises are temporary, such organizations must be easily assembled and disassembled. Individual partner organizations do not cease to exist during their membership of the VE. This point highlights another important issue, that of security. Security matters require appropriate industrial legislation and legal protection to be established.

2.4 Automation and Information Technology 自动化及通信技术

Agile manufacturing needs intelligent sensing and decision-making systems capable of automatically performing many tasks traditionally executed by human beings. Visual inspection is one such task and hence there is a need for effective automated visual inspection systems in AM environments. Agile manufacturing requires agile-enabling technologies such as virtual machine tools, flexible fixturing, and agile design alternatives. As pointed out earlier, physically distributed manufacturing environments/VEs demand high-level communication systems such as Internet, EDI and Electronic Commerce to exchange information at various levels of manufacturing organizations. Flexible fixturing is a key technology in the integration of AM and the lack of effective flexible fixturing can be a significant obstacle to implementation.

System integration in AM is complicated because of the nature of a virtual and physically distributed enterprise. To be true to its concept, AM needs to adopt the principles of all process advancements evolving out of machine tool and cutting tool technology and their related scientific fields. Some researchers examine the role of enabling processes and techniques such as CAD/CAM/CAM to reduce product development cycles. Agile manufacturing requires an intelligent Concurrent Engineering(CE) design support system that can provide rapid evaluation of engineering designs and design changes. Often, this process results in modified products that require adjustment and retooling of the manufacturing processes that produce the product.

The systems for AM should include mostly software/decision support systems for various planning and control operations including materials requirements planning, design, manufacturing resource planning, scheduling, and production planning and control. Based on the nature of AM environments, we discuss the various control systems required for AM environments. There are several computer-integrated systems that could be used for AM, some of them are as follows: (i) MRPII, (ii)Internet, CAD/CAE, (iii) ERP, (iv) Multimedia, and (v) Electronic Commerce.

3. A Framework for the Development of Agile Manufacturing 敏捷制造开发框架

In this section, a framework for the development of agile manufacturing is presented. In this framework, some of the practical issues of agility in manufacturing are addressed consistent with the modified concepts and definition of agile manufacturing. There are several tools and methods that have been proposed to develop an agile manufacturing system. For example, somebody proposed an object-oriented model of an AMS with definitions of the agile objects at four levels and their features. Furthermore, the model explains the process in which the agile objects, under the stimulation of tasks (market demands), get assembled into objects at higher levels and are integrated into agile systems by sending information to each other and by accepting information selectively. The object-oriented method can be adopted to study the agile system and its working mechanisms. The framework proposed here constitutes the following major strategies and technologies for achieving agile manufacturing: (1)Partnership formation and supplier development, (2)IT in manufacturing, (3) Enterprise Integration and Management with the help of advanced IT, (4)Virtual reality tools and techniques in manufacturing. (5)The application of most of the advanced manufacturing concepts and technologies, such as Computer-Integrated Manufacturing/Services, Manufacturing/Service Strategy, Enterprise Integration, Rapid

Prototyping, CE, New Product Development, BPR, and SCM, (6) Global manufacturing/service perspectives (physically distributed manufacturing environments) with the help of IT, such as E-Commerce, ERP, SAP, Internet, WWW, CAD/CAM, Simulation, Multimedia and MRPII.

3.1 Strategic Planning 策略计划

For virtual agile manufacturing, temporary alliances and integration of complementary core competencies is a necessity. Therefore, based on a given demand along the supply chain, there is a need to select partners based on their involvement in the value-adding chains. Development of VE requires the following: (i) a framework for the corporate strategy formulation process based on global competitiveness for manufactured goods and services, (ii) a decision support system for selecting suitable partners based on the required core competencies, (iii) an IT-based SCM system for controlling operations in VE, (iv) performance measurement system for continuous improvement in an AM environment. Existing methods and tools can be used for strategy formulation and selecting partners for AM enterprise development. Marketing research would help to identify the competitive performance objectives, based on which agile strategies can be formulated. Moreover, VR tools and techniques could be used to make a quick decision based on the more accurate data analysis.

CE within a fast-paced product development environment favors collaborative work between engineering disciplines. Certain challenges of human factors posed by the agile environment can be overcome by a series of team meetings during which the team jointly develops the project plan, including objectives, strategies for meeting objectives, a detailed task network, schedule and resource and funding projections. The information technologies alone are not sufficient to achieve the desired communications efficiency and, if anything, the unfamiliarity of the technologies could impede communications efficiency.

Agile manufacturing has different requirements for the workforce as compared with traditional systems, and they are: (i) closer interdependence among activities, (ii) different skill requirements, usually higher average skill levels, (iii) more immediate and costly consequences of any malfunction, (iv) output more sensitive to variations in human skill, knowledge and attitudes and to mental effort rather than physical effort, (v) continual change and development, and (vi) higher capital investment per employee, and favor employees responsibility for a particular product, part or process. These, to some extent, define the characteristics of an agile workforce and the training and education required, which include IT-skilled workers, knowledge in team working and negotiation and advanced manufacturing strategies and technologies, empowered employees, multifunctional workforce, multilingual workforce, and self-directed teams.

An agile organization should posses the capability of a learning organization. For this purpose, IT can be used along with a suitable organizational structure that promotes innovation and training and education. In a global manufacturing environment, the communication should be standardized for improving the cooperative supported work in a VE. This requires a standard computer-aided communication system with suitable changes to suit the local environment, such as translation into a different language. In addition, the agile manufacturing can be achieved by suitable strategic alliances based on mergers and acquisitions with the objective of obtaining required services. Other external factors, such as type of the market and products, location, government policies and environmental regulations need to be considered in the strategic planning for the suitability of AM and its development.

3.2 Product Design 产品设计

The reduction of product development cycle time is important in an agile manufacturing environment to meet the changing market requirements by suitably reconfiguring the available resources and developing suppliers. Generally, a major portion of the manufacturing cycle time is shared by product development time. Reducing the product development cycle time is a major task in AM. For this,

---

相互依存

影响 / 故障 / 敏感
变化 / 精神努力
体力努力
资本投资
责任

谈判

被授权
多功能的 / 多语种的

具有

促进 / 创新

适应

战略联盟
合并 / 收购

适应性

产品开发周期

部分

concepts/techniques such as CE, DfM, DfA, DfQ and QFD, and technologies such as CAD/CAE, Virtual Design Environment and Rapid Prototyping can be used. Even when a design firm is contracted for high quality design products/services, it still needs to interact with all other partners along the value-adding chain of the VE. In order to achieve this, a cooperation with a multidisciplinary team for reducing the overall product development cycle time is required. Online data gathering (such as E-Commerce) could be used to learn more about exact customer and market requirements.

3.3 Virtual Enterprise 虚拟企业

It is essential to develop VE in a more productive way by reducing the time and cost as well as delivering goods/services in a competitive manner in global markets. The following steps can be employed for developing a VE: (a) identify the corporate objectives, (b) based on the multiple manufacturing performance objectives, identify the product/service requirements from suppliers, (c) select partners based on the core competencies using a suitable supplier ranking system, (d) using the time scale, which should be rather short, link it as a VE with the help of automation and IT. In addition, the human resource management should be given due attention while developing VE for AM. A Data Management Framework(DMF) to support agility in manufacturing is needed. A DMF has been defined as the ability of an enterprise to manage distributed data, information, and knowledge as the decisive enabler for core enterprise business processes. The purpose of DMF is to provide a seamless enterprise data management solution in support of the AM environments. It must be stressed, however, that such seamless data integration is potentially complex. Integration of current fragmented computer systems, causing over-complexity, is perhaps the biggest challenge the AM enterprise faces.

3.4 Automation and Information Technology 自动化及通信技术

Automation and IT play a predominant role in the development of a physically distributed enterprise. The role of automation and IT can be identified in several areas of the development process.

The most important are (i) strategy formulation, (ii) tactical management, (iii) operations control and (iv) systems. For example, the concepts of AM can be validated using computer-aided simulation and a full scale-manufacturing cell. From the review of agile-enabling technologies, it can be noted that the selection of technologies for achieving agility in manufacturing depends upon the strategies that are selected to meet changing market requirements. For example, JIT may require EDI, FMS may need AGVs, Robots and NC machine tools while agility heavily relies on virtual manufacturing enterprise or physically distributed manufacturing environments. Suffice to state that technologies such as IT, manufacturing cells, robots, flexible part feeders, modular assembly hardware, automated visual inspection systems, virtual machine tools, flexible fixturing, CAD/CAM and automated high-level process planning are essential for developing agile manufacturing systems.

3.5 Aligning Agile Strategies and Technologies 调整敏捷策略和技术

We have made explicit aligning technological solutions with the business strategy so that the problems of selection, prioritization and implementation can be addressed. In addition, we show how the framework reported here can be used to develop an agile manufacturing system in practice.

Table 17.1 provides some generic guidelines for strategies and technologies with the objective of achieving agile manufacturing. For example, one of the major characteristics of an agile organization is the quick response or the speed with which it can respond to changing market requirements. It requires strategies such as alliances based on core competencies, physically distributed manufacturing environment, Supply Chain Management and technologies such as Internet, Enterprise Resource Planning(ERP) systems and SAP. Similarly, reconfigurability is an essential characteristic of agile organizations. Reconfigurability depends upon skills available and other capital resources. GEC Marconi Aerospace (GECMAe) implemented certain agile technologies with the objective of improving the agility in the organization. For example, GECMAe has implemented CE and EDI for improving the quality of design and to minimize the total cycle for manufacturing aerospace products.

Table 17.1 Linking Agile Strategies With Technologies 连接敏捷策略与技术

Agile enterprise characteristics 敏捷企业特征	Strategies 策略	Technologies 技术
Quick Response Manufacturing 快速响应制造	Virtual Enterprise 虚拟企业, Supplier development, Partnership development	Rapid Prototyping 快速原型, Internet, WWW, E-mail
Flexible Organization 柔性组织	Group technology(GT) 成组技术, Manufacturing Cells 制造单元, Concurrent Engineering 并行工程	Robots, AGVs 自动导引小车, NC Machines, CAD, CAPP, and CIM
Learning Organization 学习组织	Matrix Organizational Structure, Strategic Alliances 战略联盟, Systems Thinking, Knowledge Management 知识管理, Empowerment 授权, Team Work	Information Technology, Groupware 群件, Internet, E-Commerce 电子商务, Multimedia
Integrated Value Chain 集成价值链	Supplier Development 供应商开发	MRP, ERP, SAP, Internet, E-Commerce
Physically Distributed Manufacturing Environment 物理分布式制造环境	Lean Manufacturing 精益制造, FMS and JIT 柔性制造系统与及时生产	Knowledge workers, Learning Organization
Mass Customization 大批量定制	Flexible Resources 柔性资源	GT, EDI 电子数据交换, CAD/CAM/CAPP, E-Commerce
Reconfigurability 可重构	Virtual Enterprise 虚拟企业, Flexible Resources	CE 并行工程, STEP 产品数据交换标准, CIM

4. Summary 总结

Two key characteristics of manufacturing companies discussed in this chapter are 'Agility' – the ability of a company to effect changes in its systems, structure and organization – and 'Responsiveness' – the ability of a company to gather information from its commercial environment and to detect and anticipate changes, to recover from changes and to improve as a result of change. Manufacturing companies, even those operating in relatively stable conditions with good market positions, are facing fast and often unanticipated changes in their commercial environment. Being agile in such environments means being flexible, cost effective, productive and producing with consistent high quality. Each company will respond in a specific and different way deploying its own agile characteristics. The problem of identifying, analysing and evaluating agility is that no commonly accepted practical frame of reference or analytical structure exists.

The literature available on an AM workforce is rather limited. The reason for this is that there is no clear-cut framework for identifying the implications of AM on workforce characteristics, and most of the literature deals with enabling technologies and some strategies of AM. However, human factors play a significant role in the successful development and implementation of AM. The key issues of human factors that need to be considered in agile environment are knowledge workers, multilingual workforce, multinational workforce, incentive schemes, type and level of education and training, relation with unions, and pay award.

Most of the available systems (control and information) are developed for traditional manufacturing environments where a static market behavior and resources have been employed for producing goods and services. The support systems for AMS rely heavily on computer-based information systems such as EDI, Internet and Electronic Commerce. Therefore, a flexible architecture for systems to accommodate temporary alliances will help improve enterprise integration and hence agility in organizations.

专业词汇

agile manufacturing(AM) 敏捷制造
lean manufacturing 精益制造
reconfigurability 可重构
concurrent engineering (CE) 并行工程
virtual reality (VR) 虚拟现实
business process reengineering (BPR) 业务流程重组

one-of-a-kind product
一种类型只有一个，单件小批量产品
subcontractors 分包商
virtual enterprise (VM) 虚拟企业
complementary competencies 互补优势
strategic planning 战略规划
rapid prototyping (RP) 快速原型
STEP (standard for the exchange of product model data) 产品模型数据交互标准
group technology (GT) 成组技术
virtual manufacturing (VM) 虚拟制造
intelligent sensing 智能传感
visual inspection 视觉检测
virtual machine tools 虚拟机床
flexible fixturing 柔性夹具
EDI (Electronic Data Interchange) 电子数据交换
electronic commerce (EC) 电子商务

supply chain management(SCM)
供应链管理
SAP 德国 SAP 公司的 ERP 软件
simulation 仿真
decision support system
决策支持系统
DfM (design for manufacturability)
面向制造的设计
DfA (design for assembly)
面向装配的设计
DfQ (design for quality)
面向质量的设计
QFD (quality function deployment)
质量功能展开
human resource management
人力资源管理

思考题：

1. 什么是敏捷制造？它有哪些特征？
2. 敏捷制造包括哪些策略和技术？
3. 什么是虚拟企业？如何实现和开发一个虚拟企业？
4. 在敏捷制造中需要用到哪些自动化和通信技术？
5. 什么是并行工程？它有何特征？

Chapter 18 Remanufacturing
再制造

1. Introduction 介绍

Traditionally, products have been designed and manufactured to meet functional needs during the product's useful lifetime, with little regard for the product's end-of-life. Recently, in response to stricter environmental legislation, particularly in Europe and parts of Asia, that assigns responsibility for products at the end-of-life to manufacturers, more products have been designed for ease of scrap-material recycling. Scrap-material recycling involves separating a product into different materials and reprocessing the materials for use in similar or degraded applications.

For appropriate products, remanufacturing offers significant environmental and economic benefits over scrap-material recycling. Remanufacturing involves recycling at the parts level as opposed to the material level. Recycling at the higher level of components avoids resource consumption for possibly unnecessary reprocessing of material. Remanufacturing also postpones the repeated degradation of the raw material through contamination and molecular breakdown, frequently characteristic of scrap-material recycling. Furthermore, remanufacturing can divert parts that are not recyclable for material content from landfill and incineration. The production-batch nature of the remanufacturing process enables it to salvage functionally failed but repairable products that are discarded due to high labor costs associated with individual repair.

The relationship between manufacturing and remanufacturing is depicted in Fig. 18.1, which shows that while the manufacturing process produces new products, the remanufacturing process can repeatedly take products at the end-of-life and transform them to a "like-new" condition for reuse. A few manufacturers remanufacture their own products. In the office equipment market, companies such as the Xerox Corporation have achieved $200 million in annual savings by remanufacturing their photocopiers. Some manufacturers, such as the Ford Motor Company have authorized remanufacturers to process after-market parts for their cars. With increasing international product take-back legislation, more manufacturers are likely to become interested in the remanufacture of their products.

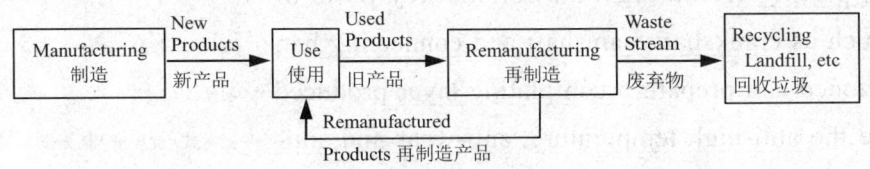

Fig. 18.1 Relationship between Manufacturing and Remanufacturing

Lund (1996) compiled a list of 9,903 remanufacturers and identified the most dominant product sectors as automotive, electrical apparatus, tires, and toner cartridges. The automotive sector, with typical products of alternators, starter motors, water pumps, clutches and engines, comprises the highest percentage, 46% of Lund's database. Next are electrical apparatus (transformers, electrical motors, switch gear) at 23%, toner cartridges at 14% and retreaded tires at 12%. Other categories comprise 5% of Lund's database of remanufacturers.

2. Remanufacturing Technologies 再制造技术

Surface engineering technologies are the key part of remanufacture. People successfully developed advanced nano-surface engineering technology and auto-surface engineering technology. The former makes full use of the small size effect of nano particles so as to greatly increase the surface performance of remanufactured products, the latter meets the exigent need of batch production and automatic production in remanufacture and consequently greatly raise the quality of remanufactured products.

2.1 Nano-surface Engineering Technology 纳米表面工程技术

Micro-nano technology is one of the three high and new technologies in 21st century. It will take thirty to forty years to realize the application of the integral nano technology. At present, people integrate nano materials and traditional surface engineering technologies by way of distributing or compounding nano-particles in surface coatings homogeneously, whereby people developed nano-surface engineering technology with independent intellectual property rights, among which the typical technology is compound nano-particle brush plating technology. As for the key parts of automobile engine such as crankshaft, camshaft and connecting bar, the technology mentioned can prepare brush plating layer produced with greatly improve the anti-high temperature, anti-wear and anti-fatigue performances of these parts. Particularly noticeable, this technology meets the demand to remanufacture of the engine blades of the imported aircrafts so as to enhance the anti-micro-friction of blades significantly, which was proved by 300h bench test and the cost is only 1/10 of the maintenance expense of the introduced technology from some foreign country. Up to now, nano-brush plating technology has been widely applied in China and has played an important role in maintenance and remanufacture field.

2.2 Active Self-repair Additive Technology 主动自修复添加技术

Active self-repair additive technology can form solid repair film to conduct antifriction, lubrication and self-repairing on friction surface of engines by means of tribochemistry effect, and help to realize a dynamic balance between friction and repair so as to realize and self-repairing without even stopping and disintegrating the engine. This technology has obtained independent intellectual property rights. The results of 300h durable bench test concerning M6 active self-repair additive in 6 cylinders Jeep engines show that this additive increases the engine power by 6%, enhances the torque by 2%, and reduces the oil consumption by 6%. Still the 15000 kilometers application test of the additive in 3 buses of Qingdao city shows that it can raise the engine output power by 2% – 5%, save fuel oil by 3% – 6% and cut down tail gas discharge by 30% – 50%. In addition, the one year and a half proving test in 20 heavy-duty vehicles indicates that the tightness between piston and cylinder is improved, the original burning oil appearance of engines turns better obviously, the life-span of engine oil extends by 50%, and the oil change period is doubled.

2.3 Auto-surface Engineering Technology 自动表面工程技术

Auto high velocity arc spray(HVAS) technology uses the operating machine to hold the spray gun, realize the route planning of the spray process by programming, control the spray processing parameters through real-time feedback and to complete the automatic spray process according to the set route. This technology is suitable for remanufacture of important parts of the heavy-duty vehicles such as the engine cylinders and crankshaft case. The remanufacture time of one single engine case drops from one and half hours with manual labor to twenty minutes by automatic process, the efficiency increased by 3.5 times. As for the remanufacture of crankshaft, cylinder and other parts, the consumption of material is only 0.5% of weight of the part itself and the cost is no more than 1/10 of the price of the new product. In addition, the process of crankshaft remanufacture lacks the 8 hours' carbonitriding procedure which is required during new products manufacture, so it will save vast energy resources.

Auto-nano-particle composite brush plating technology realizes the automation of brush plating process by solving the key problems such as the continuous supply, recycling and the real-time monitoring during plating. The special auto-nano-particle composite brush plating machine for the remanufacture of engine connecting rods has been developed. This machine can complete the brush plating work of 4 – 6 connecting rods at the same time and make the operation time of a single rod shortens from 60 minutes to 5 minutes, so the efficiency increases as much as 10 times. The consumption of energy resources and materials for remanufacture of one piece of connecting rod is only 50% and 10% respectively of that of a new one and the cost is just 1/10. In general, the resistance to wear of auto-nano-particle composite brush plated connecting rod is 1.4 – 1.8 times of that of their manual counterparts.

Semi-automatic micro plasma arc (MPA) cladding technology shows the features of high current density and small thermal input, so it will solve the problem of distortion due to large thermal input which is typical of traditional arc welding, especially in small parts and components. Moreover, because of metallurgical bonding between cladding layer and substrate, remanufactured parts can resist impact and cyclic loading. According to previous repair specifications of engines, engine valve has to be out of service when the abrasion of its sealing cone is out of tolerance. With MPA cladding technology, it can be possible to remanufacture the waste and old engine valves. After remanufacture, the distortion is small, surface hardness comes back to the value before abrasion, and the quality of remanufactured valves is better than that of a new one. From economy's points of view, a new engine valve is 70 Yuan, but a remanufactured valve is only 10 Yuan. At present, the three technologies mentioned above have been applied in the engines remanufacture production line of Ji'nan Fuqiang Remanufacture Company that is one of the national initial demonstration and pilot enterprises for remanufacture.

3. Remanufacturing Process for Automotive Engines
汽车发动机再制造过程

At the original-equipment remanufacturer (OER) of automotive engines, the production-batch process proceeds as follows. The received engines are delivered to the disassembly station. In each batch, seven to fifteen engines, depending on the size of the engine, are disassembled. The engines are dismantled and the parts sorted into baskets for cleaning. The cleaning process uses either chemical spray or high-pressure water. The processes for the different parts are as follows.

Block – After a cleaning process that removes grease and other chemicals from engine blocks, the bore diameters are measured using gauges and compared to specifications. For blocks within specification, threads are tapped before the blocks are sent to machining lines. The bores for the crankshafts are checked for straightness and size, and machining is performed as necessary. Next, the seat is milled and the piston housing is bored. Finally, the blocks are washed to remove metal chips accumulated during the machining processes and await delivery to the assembly line.

Cylinder Head – Cylinder heads disassembled from engine blocks proceed to a subsequent station for further disassembly of the springs, rocker arms, valve pins, etc. The aluminum cylinder heads are then washed in a separate machine since they cannot be treated together with iron and steel parts. The cylinder heads are then sand blasted before threads are tapped. Next, guides for the valve pins and valve seats are replaced before seat cutting or milling is performed. Like the engine blocks, cylinder heads are washed to remove excess metal chips accumulated during machining before proceeding to assembly.

Crankshaft – After being cleaned together with camshafts, connecting rods, oil pans and valve covers, crankshafts are delivered to machining lines. The crankshafts are first gauged to check the dimensions of all shafts. When a part satisfies all the specifications, it proceeds to stations for grinding and polishing. Crankshafts are gauged again before being delivered to the assembly line.

Camshaft – The process for camshafts is similar to that for crankshafts. They are cleaned, gauged, ground and polished. However, after cleaning, instead of proceeding to a machining line, they are brought to a station where usually one employee is responsible for all the remaining processes to be performed on a particular camshaft.

Connecting Rod – There is no machining process in use for connecting rods. After cleaning, all connecting rods are delivered to a station where they are sorted according to engine model. Then, all rods from the same engine type will be loaded onto a shaft that serves as an initial measuring tool. If a rod cannot fit onto the shaft, it is scrapped because the attached cap is likely mismatched. All bolts are replaced before the connecting rods are gauged to check dimensions. Finally, connecting rods are weighed and grouped by weight. Depending on the number required by the engine type, four to eight rods with the same weight, within an accepted tolerance, are grouped together to enhance crankshaft performance.

Oil Pan/Valve Cover – Comparatively, the refurbishment of

oil pans/valve covers requires simpler processes. After cleaning, accessible <u>dents</u> are removed from the oil pans/valve covers. If the <u>convex side</u> of the dent is inaccessible, the dent cannot be removed and the pan/cover will be <u>scrapped</u>. The oil pans/valve covers are then painted before proceeding to assembly.

  Cylinder Sleeve – After cleaning, cylinder sleeves are <u>sand blasted</u>. The <u>bores</u> are then <u>gauged</u> and the <u>seats</u> polished. Lastly, the cylinder sleeves are <u>bored</u>. Special care must be taken during the boring process and consequently a considerable number of sleeves are machined <u>oversized</u>.

凹痕
凸边
废弃

缸套/喷砂
孔/度量/气门座
转孔

过大

专业词汇

environmental legislation 环境立法
scrap-material recycling 废旧材料回收
degradation 降解
contamination 污染
landfill 垃圾填埋场
incineration 焚化
electrical apparatus 电气设备
tire 轮胎
toner cartridges 硒鼓
alternator 交流发电机
clutch 离合器
surface engineering 表面工程
brush plating 电刷镀
crankshaft case 曲轴箱
camshaft 凸轮轴
anti-wear 抗磨损
anti-fatigue 抗疲劳
antifriction 耐磨
lubrication 润滑

tribochemistry 摩擦化学
engine cylinder 发动机气缸
carbonitriding 碳氮共渗
micro plasma arc cladding technology 微等离子弧覆层技术
metallurgical bonding 冶金结合
abrasion 磨损
disassemble 分解
dismantle 拆卸
engine block 发动机缸体
gauge 量具
piston housing 活塞室
cylinder head 缸盖
grinding 磨削
polishing 抛光
valve cover 气门盖
refurbishment 翻新
cylinder sleeve 气缸套
sand blasted 喷砂

思考题：

1. 什么是再制造？它与传统制造有何区别与联系？
2. 再制造技术有何益处？
3. 常用的再制造技术有哪些？请简要解释说明。
4. 请描述发动机零件的再制造过程。

Chapter 19　Green Manufacturing
绿色制造

1. Introduction 介绍

There are many ways industrial facilities can implement technologies and workplace practices to improve the environmental outcomes of their production processes and many motivations for doing so. Green manufacturing can lead to lower raw material costs, production efficiency gains, reduced environmental and occupational safety expenses, and improved corporate image.

In general, green manufacturing involves production processes which use inputs with relatively low environmental impacts, which are highly efficient, and which generate little or no waste or pollution. Green manufacturing encompasses source reduction, recycling, and green product design. Source reduction is broadly defined to include any actions reducing the waste initially generated. Recycling includes using or reusing wastes as ingredients in a process or as an effective substitute for a commercial product, or returning the waste to the original process which generated it as a substitute for raw material. Green product design involves creating products whose design, composition, and usage minimize their environmental impacts throughout their lifecycle.

Source reduction and recycling activities already have been widely adopted by industrial facilities. According to 1993 U.S. Environmental Protection Agency Biennial Reporting System data, which cover facilities generating large quantities of hazardous waste, 57% and 43% of these facilities had begun, expanded or previously implemented source reduction and recycling, respectively. According to a 1995 survey of over 200 U.S. manufacturing companies, 90% of them cited source reduction and 86% cited recycling as main elements in their pollution prevention plans.

2. Organizing for Green Manufacturing 绿色制造组织

Green manufacturing provides many opportunities for cost reduction, meeting environmental standards, and contributing to an improved corporate image. But finding and exploiting these opportunities frequently involve more technological problems. The ten most frequently cited waste minimization actions reported by large hazardous waste generators are listed in Table 19.1.

企业形象 / 利用

危险的

常用的危险废弃物最小化行动

Table 19.1 Most Frequently Cited Hazardous Waste Minimization Actions

Percent of All Action 行动百分比	Waste Minimization Action 废弃物最小化行动
8.9%	Improved maintenance schedule, recordkeeping or procedures 改善维护计划、记录保存和工艺
8.0%	Other changes in operating practices(not involving changes in equipment) 在操作实践中的其他改变
7.1%	Substituted raw materials 替代原材料
6.5%	Source reduction activity 资源减少行为
5.1%	Stopped combining hazardous and non-hazardous waste 停止组合危险和不危险的废弃物
4.8%	Modified equipment, layout, or piping 修改设备、布局和管道
4.6%	Other process modifications 其他的工艺修改
4.4%	Instituted better controls on operating conditions 设立更好的操作环境控制
4.1%	Ensured that materials not in inventory past shelf-life 确保材料不在库存中超过保质期
4.0%	Changed to aqueous cleaners 使用水性清洁剂

As the data show, only a small portion of these actions involve new or modified technology. Most involve improving operating practices or controls, or fairly basic ideas – like waste segregation or raw material changes – that production workers can suggest and implement. Thus, it is first necessary to organize production operations, management functions, and personnel for green manufacturing to facilitate the identification and development of both technical and common-sense waste minimization ideas.

There are several important prerequisites for this process. First,

废弃物分离

常识性的

先决条件

it is critical to have an accounting of inputs, wastes, and their associated costs at each point in the production process. According to 1994 EPA data, 31% of all reported source reduction actions were first identified through pollution prevention opportunity or materials balance audits. The normal financial incentives to reduce costs can be highly efficient within such an accounting system, but the actual efficiency greatly depends on the extent to which true costs accounting for. The pinpointing of costs, particularly tracking them back to specific production processes, and the projection of future costs are challenging.

Second, the facility must know the environmental laws with which it must comply now and in the foreseeable future. This includes environmental permits specifically applicable to it. The facility also must assess the legal implications of possible changes in its operations.

Third, green manufacturing must be a central concern of the facility's top management. This is usually helped by outside pressure, or by the convincing demonstration of its benefits.

Fourth, it is typically very helpful to involve production workers in green manufacturing. When they are involved in the environmental implications of their activities, they often make substantial contributions, especially improvements in industrial housekeeping, internal recycling, and limited changes in production processes. According to 1994 EPA data, 42% of all reported source reduction activities were first identified through management or employee recommendations.

Fifth, green manufacturing will greatly benefit from the easy availability of technical and environmental information about clever technology options. Both in-house technical and environmental experts and outside consultants can be useful. It also can be desirable to involve the facility's suppliers and customers in the effort. Often they can provide solutions not easily perceived by the facility involved in the actual production.

Finally, challenging objectives and monitoring of the facility's progress towards achieving them can help in creating effective green manufacturing. The targets may be financial, physical, legal, and personnel.

3. Choosing Green Manufacturing Options 绿色制造选项

Once the proper organizational approach is established, the first step in choosing options for green manufacturing is making an inventory by production operation of the inputs used (e.g., energy, raw materials, water, etc.) and the wastes generated. These wastes include off-specification products, inputs returned to their suppliers, solid wastes, and other non-product outputs sent to treatment or disposal facilities or discharged into the environment.

The second step is selecting the most important non-product outputs or waste streams to focus upon. Their relative importance could depend upon the costs involved, environmental and occupational safety impacts, legal requirements, public pressures, or a combination thereof.

The third step is generating options to reduce these non-product outputs at their origin. These options fall into five general categories: product changes, process changes, input changes, increased internal re-use of wastes, and better housekeeping.

The fourth step is to pragmatically evaluate the options for their environmental advantage, technical feasibility, economic sufficiency, and employee acceptability. With respect to economic sufficiency, calculating the pay-back period is usually adequate.

This evaluation usually leads to a number of options, especially in better housekeeping and input changes, which are environmentally advantageous, easy to implement, and financially desirable. Thus, the fifth step is to rapidly implement such options. There typically also are other options which take longer to evaluate, but which usually lead to a substantial number which are worth implementing.

4. Potential Green Manufacturing Options
潜在的绿色制造选项

The options for green manufacturing can be divided into five major area: product changes, production process changes, changes of inputs in the production process, internal re-use of wastes, and better housekeeping. The following discussion focuses on the physical nature of changes which can be implemented.

Changes in production processes. Many major production process changes fall into the following categories: (1) changing dependence on human intervention, (2) use of a continuous instead of a batch process, (3) changing the nature of the steps in the production process, (4) eliminating steps in the production process, (5) changing cleaning processes.

Production dependent on active human intervention has a significant failure rate. This may lead to various problems, ranging from off-specification products to major accidents. A strategy that can reduce the dependence of production processes on active human intervention is having machines take over parts of what humans used to do. Automated process control, robots used for welding purposes, and numerically controlled cutting all may reduce wastes.

With respect to using a continuous, rather than batch process, the former consistently causes less environmental impact than the latter. This is due to the reduction of residuals in the production machinery and thus the reduced need for cleaning, and better opportunities for process control, allowing for improved resource and energy efficiency and decreasing off-specification products. There are, however, opportunities for environmentally improved technology in batch processes. For chemical batch processes, for instance, the main waste prevention methods are (1) eliminate or minimize unwanted byproducts, possibly by changing reactants, processes, or equipment, (2) recycle the solvents used in reactions and extractions, and (3) recycle excess reactants. Furthermore, careful design and well-planned use can also minimize residuals to be cleaned away when batch processes are involved.

Changing the nature of steps in a production process – whether physical, chemical, or biological – can considerably affect its environmental impact. Such changes may involve switching from one chemical process to another, or from a chemical to a physical or biological process, or vice versa. In general, using a more selective production route – such as through inorganic catalysts and enzymes –

will be environmentally beneficial by reducing inputs and their associated wastes. Switching from a chemical to a physical production process also may be beneficial. For example, the banning of chlorofluorocarbons led to other ways of producing flexible polyurethane foams. One resulting process was based on the controlled use of variable pressure, where carbon dioxide and water blow the foam, with the size of the foam cells depending on the pressure applied. An example of an environmentally beneficial change in the physical nature of a process is using electrodynamics in spraying. A major problem of spraying processes is that a significant amount of sprayed material misses its target. In such cases, waste may be greatly reduced by giving the target and the sprayed material opposite electrical charges.

Eliminating steps in the production process may prevent wastes because each step typically creates wastes. For example, facilities have developed processes that eliminated several painting steps. These cut costs and reduce the paint used and thus emissions and waste. In the chemical industry, there is a trend to eliminate neutralization steps which generate waste salts as byproducts. This is mainly achieved by using a more selective type of synthesis.

Cleaning is the source of considerable environmental impacts from production processes. These impacts can partly be reduced by changing inputs in the cleaning process (e.g., using water-based cleaners, rather than solvents). Also, production processes can be changed so that the need for cleaning is reduced or eliminated, such as in the microelectronics industry, where improved production techniques have sharply reduced the need for cleaning with organic solvents. Sometimes, by careful consideration of production sequences, the need for cleaning can be eliminated, such as in textile printing, where good planning of printing sequences may eliminate the need for cleaning away residual pigments. In other processes, reduced cleaning is achieved by minimizing carry-over from one process step to the next. The switch from batch to continuous processes will also usually reduce the need for cleaning.

Changes of inputs in the production process. Changes in inputs is an important tool in green manufacturing. Both major and minor product ingredients and inputs which contribute to production, without being incorporated in the end product, may be worth changing. An example where changing a minor input in production may substantially reduce its environmental impact is the use of paints in the production of cars and airplanes. The introduction of powder-based and high solids paints substantially reduces the emission of volatile organic compounds. Also, substituting water-based for solvent-based coatings may lessen environmental impacts.

Internal re-use. The potential for internal re-use is often substantial, with many possibilities for the re-use of water, energy, and some chemicals and metals. Washing, heating, and cooling in a counter-current process will facilitate the internal re-use of energy and water. Closed-loop process water recycling which replaces single pass systems is usually economically attractive, with both water and chemicals potentially being recycled. In some production processes there may be possibilities for cascade-type re-use, in which water used in one process step is used in another process step where quality requirements are less stringent. Similarly, energy may be used in a cascade-type way where waste heat from high temperature processes is used to meet demand for lower temperature heat.

Better housekeeping. Good housekeeping refers to generally simple, routinized, non-resource intensive measures that keep a facility in good working and environmental order. It includes segregating wastes, minimizing chemical and waste inventories, installing overflow alarms and automatic shutoff valves, eliminating leaks and drips and putting colleting devices at places where spills may occur frequent inspections aimed at identifying environmental concerns and potential malfunctionings of the production process, instituting better controls on operating conditions, regular fine-tuning of machinery, and optimizing maintenance schedules. These types of actions often offer relatively quick, easy, and inexpensive ways to reduce chemical and wastes.

专业词汇

green manufacturing 绿色制造
production process 生产工艺
environmental impact 环境影响
ingredient 成分
feedstock 原料
hazardous waste 危险废物
waste segregation 废物分离
off-specification 不合规格的
disposal facilities 处理设施
discharge 排出
occupational safety 职业安全
physical nature 物理性质
intervention 干预
inorganic 无机的

catalysts 催化剂
enzymes 酶
electrodynamics 电动力学
spraying 喷射
emission 排放
neutralization 中和
byproduct 副产品
synthesis 合成
organic solvent 有机溶剂
volatile organic compounds
挥发性有机化合物
shutoff valve 截止阀
malfunctioning 故障

思考题：

1. 什么是绿色制造？绿色制造有何益处？
2. 在生产中采取哪些行为可以产生最少废弃物？
3. 简述开展绿色制造的步骤。
4. 潜在的绿色制造选项包括哪些内容？请简要说明各部分内容。

参考文献

[1] 施平. 先进制造技术. 哈尔滨：哈尔滨工业大学出版社，2006.

[2] 马玉录，刘东学. 机械设计制造及其自动化专业英语. 第二版. 北京：化学工业出版社，2009.

[3] 高成秀. 机械工程专业英语. 北京：电子工业出版社，2010.

[4] 唐一平. 先进制造技术（英文版）. 第三版. 哈尔滨：科学出版社，2012.

[5] 施平. 机械工程专业英语. 第 14 版. 哈尔滨工业大学出版社，2012.

[6] 朱世强，王宣银. 机器人技术及其应用. 杭州：浙江大学出版社，2000.

[7] F. 罗伯特·雅各布斯，理查德.B. 蔡斯. 运营管理. 任建标译注. 北京：机械工业出版社，2011.

[8] ISO Standard 8373: Manipulating Industrial Robots-Vocabulary, 1994.

[9] Benjamin Caldwell, Gregory M. Mocko. Product Data Management in Undergraduate Education. Proceedings of the ASME 2008 International Design Engineering Technical Conferences & Computers and Information in Engineering Conference (IDETC/CIE2008), August 3-6, 2008, Brooklyn, New York, USA

[10] Tijjani Adama, U. Hashima, Sutiknob, Th. S. Dhahia and T. Nazwaa. Material Engineering for Nano Structure Formation: Fabrication and characterization. 2012 International Conference on Advances Science and Contemporary Engineering (ICASCE 2012), Procedia Engineering, 2012, pp.361-368

[11] Computer integrated manufacturing systems. http://www.gobookee.org/computer-integrated-manufacturing-systems/

[12] Michael McClellan. Introduction to Manufacturing Execution Systems. MES Conference & Exposition, Baltimore Maryland, 2001

[13] MESA International. The Benefits of MES: A Report From the Field. Pittsburgh, PA, USA

[14] Jens J. Dahlgaard. Lean production, six sigma quality, TQM and company culture. The TQM Magazine, 2006, Vol.18, No.3, pp.263-281

[15] A. Gunasekarany and Y. Y. Yusufz. Agile manufacturing: a taxonomy of strategic and technological imperatives. International Journal of Production Research, 2002, Vol.40, No.6, 1357-1385

[16] A. Lam, M. Sherwood, L. H. Shu. FMEA-based Design for Remanufacture Using Automotive-Remanufacturer Data. http://www.mie.utoronto.ca/labs/lcdlab/shu/ pubs/Lam_etal_SAE_01.pdf

[17] Mark Atlas and Richard Florida. Green Manufaturing. Handbook of Technology Management, 1998, http://www.creativeclass.com

[18] J Dutta Majumdar and I Manna. Laser processing of materials. Sadhana, Vol.28, Parts 3 & 4, June/August 2003, pp495-562